Praise for
Using the Power of Hope to Cope with Dying

"This potent and inspiring message is highly recommended for both the professional and the nonprofessional end-of-life caregiver."
—Dolores Krieger, Ph.D., R.N., author of *Therapeutic Touch as Transpersonal Healing*

"When a person is dying, the sense of having lost all hope is often worse than the prospect of death; this book is an antidote to hopelessness."
—Ira Byock, M.D., palliative care physician; author of *Dying Well* and *The Four Things That Matter Most*

"Hope is necessary for survival. It is not about statistics and there is no false hope. This book gives the reader an excellent perspective about the role hope can play in one's life while confronting one's mortality. You can learn to live until you die rather than be dying."
—Bernie Siegel, M.D., author of *Love, Medicine & Miracles* and *Help Me to Heal*

"I have just finished reading your manuscript.... It is an interesting and moving contribution to the huge literature on death."
—Elisabeth Kübler-Ross, M.D., author of *On Death and Dying*, who got a chance to read the working manuscript for this book prior to her own death in 2004.

"Rabindranath Tagore, the great Indian poet, said, 'Hope is the bird that sings before the dawn.' In this wonderful book, Cathleen Fanslow-Brunjes helps us recognize this song so we can harmonize with it. It is when the darkness is the most profound that hope emerges as the true reality. She gives us tools which we can use to create the music of love which each soul needs."
—Gladys Taylor McGarey, M.D., M.D.(H)., Founder and Past President of the American Holistic Medical Association

USING THE POWER OF HOPE TO COPE WITH DYING

The Four Stages of Hope

CATHLEEN FANSLOW–BRUNJES, M.A., R.N.

Sanger, California

Printed in the United States of America.

Published by
Quill Driver Books/Word Dancer Press, Inc.,
1254 Commerce Way, Sanger, CA 93657
559-876-2170 / 800-497-4909
QuillDriverBooks.com

Quill Driver Books' titles may be purchased for educational, fund-raising, business or promotional use. Please contact Special Markets, Quill Driver Books/Word Dancer Press, Inc. at the above address or phone numbers.

Quill Driver Books/Word Dancer Press Project Cadre:
Doris Hall, Christine Hernandez, Dave Marion,
Stephen Blake Mettee, Cassandra Williams

First Printing

ISBN 1-884956-80-7 •978-1884956-80-5

**To order a copy of this book, please call
1-800-497-4909.**

To my father,
without whom I would not be who I am,
and to my three teachers:
Dolores Krieger, Ph.D., R.N.;
Elisabeth Kübler-Ross M.D.;
and Dora Kunz

Library of Congress Cataloging-in-Publication Data

Fanslow-Brunjes, Cathleen, 1939-
Using the power of hope to cope with dying : the four stages of hope /
by Cathleen Fanslow-Brunjes.
p. cm.
ISBN 978-1-884956-80-5
1. Death—Psychological aspects. 2. Hope—Psychological aspects. I.
Title.
HQ1073.F36 2008
155.9'37—dc22

2008003483

Contents

Hope is the thing with feathers
that perches in the soul
and sings the tune without the words
and never stops at all...

—Emily Dickinson

Foreword

*H*ope is a powerful word. It is a word used by all of us in many different ways and with many different meanings. The *American Heritage College Dictionary* defines *hope* in one way as "to wish for something with expectation of its fulfillment, to expect and desire." But hope is different from wishing for something or being positive about events in your life, whatever form those events may take.

Hope is everywhere. Think about your family and your friends. Recall the way in which each one has dealt with life's experiences. Every one of us has our own way...a story about how we hope and what hope means to us. Hope is an integral part of our life and follows us as we experience life and death. It gives us a way to deal with what has happened to us.

This book, authored by my longtime friend and colleague, Cathleen Fanslow, is about helping those facing death, something many fear and do not wish to think about. It provides a powerful tool to help the dying and their family and loved ones cope with the inevitable act of dying. Those of us who began our careers in the early sixties and continue to practice today have seen many changes in the way health care is practiced and death is addressed.

This book about using the power of hope to cope with dying evolved from the author's many years of personal experiences caring for the sick and terminally ill. It draws on both what patients taught a young practitioner before the days of hospice care and on the approaches to terminal care available today. What better way to help each of us as we experience the loss of our loved ones and address our own mortality?

This book is about hope and how it will help you to confront the reality that death will eventually occur to all of us. It provides a meaningful and simple approach to the experience of dying.

Carol Reed Ash, Ed.D., R.N., FAAN
Professor Emeritus, University of Florida
Editor, *Cancer Nursing*

Acknowledgments

I would like to thank Candace Lyle Hogan who inspired me initially and helped me hear my voice in writing and Lester Hoffman whose help in refining the proposal and sample chapters was invaluable. I would also like to thank Janet Macrae, my faithful friend, who encouraged and supported me every step of the way; Kate Poss whose typing and editing skills made it come together; and Steve Mettee and his staff at Quill Driver Books whose remarkable skill at editing and refining my work made this dream become a reality.

For so many years my family, friends, colleagues, and above all my students, have been asking me to please finish my book, constantly saying, "We need it." I thank you for all your patience and support and I hope that this is just what you have been hoping for. Finally I want to thank all the patients and their loved ones who have been my teachers and my inspiration.

Introduction
The Meaning of Hope

When I became a registered nurse in 1964, before the era of hospice and patient-centered care, those with a terminal illness eked out their last days largely forgotten within a hospital's cold walls. These were the days before Elisabeth Kübler-Ross's landmark book, *On Death and Dying*, brought them out of the darkness; the days when the dying person was placed in a room at the end of the hall like an unmentionable, rarely referred to by name—it was always "the cancer in room 44" or "the heart attack in 27."

Because we in the medical profession could not cure them, the fact that they continued to die flew in the face of our thinking that we should be able to control everything. So it was, *If I can't cure you, I'm going to put you at that end room....* I can't tell you how many fights I had during that time, when doctors talked about, "Oh, the bladder cancer in room 306"— no name, no person, just a diagnosis and a room number. I wondered, *what does that do to the person?* Terminal illness had robbed them of a well-functioning body, and now the doctor strips them of their selfhood and identity. Early on, I saw how the abandonment of the dying begins.

And I can't tell you how many altercations I had over it. I'll never forget this one young doctor whom I heard talking this way. I was still in my floor-length white nun's habit (with the under cap and bonnet that allowed for absolutely no peripheral vision), the old kind that came out of the laundry starched out to *here!* So there I was in my thick white belt and cuff links with a silver cross, but that didn't stop me from acting out my rowdy nature. I'm from Brooklyn, after all, and I fancied myself a champion of the underdog, so when I heard this doctor talking as if a dying patient were not a person, I came bustling down the hall at him like a white hot fury. I stepped on his foot and grabbed his tie, and said, "How dare you! That is not just simply a diagnosis or a room number, that's a person—and what is that person's name?"

What Elisabeth Kübler-Ross, who was a psychiatrist and a doctor (and also my teacher when I began), brought into the medically dominated, cure-oriented world of that time was a new framework of thinking about the dying. She insisted on acknowledging what the terminally ill were going through psychologically. But she, as well as I, always sensed that there was something more going on than psychology, something deeper, but we weren't able to name it then.

Kübler-Ross attempted to give patients some kind of control over their fate by helping them understand the psychodynamic shifts they were going through. By classifying these shifts—naming them "the stages of grief"—she identified the psychological behaviors of the dying person and the coping mechanisms they used from diagnosis through death.

Her first stage is *Denial*: *No, no, not me.* Then *Anger* comes in: *Why me?* The anger stage is followed by the *Bargaining* stage: *Yes me, but...* The next stage is *Depression*: *Oh my god, I'm going to die.* And finally, *Acceptance*, the final stage: *I'm going to die, and somehow it's all right.* What she did was identify behaviors, and, thankfully, that alone sparked a revolution in how we thought about the process of death and how people in the medical profession treated the dying. But we both realized, as revolutionary as this was, it was just a start.

The psychodynamics reflect only a part of the dying person's experience. What was left was unearthing their own hope system, where they really live.

I knew there was something different than just this set of psychodynamics, something else going on at a deeper level than the psychological, something even more dynamic and powerful than psychological theories could explain. Eventually, over years of observation and being at the bedside, I was able to give it a name: *Hope*, a term not unfamiliar to the medical establishment even then, and a concept that has come to intrigue the academics more and more in the context of end-of-life care.

Hope is universally understood to mean something more profound than simply a wish or a goal. But it's not a loaded word so far, since it has escaped religious or spiritual connotations, and therefore people can consider it regardless of their belief system. I found that by addressing hope as the key underlying dynamic within each person that it really is , I could facilitate a dying person's entree into the powerful force of healing that was already within them. Time and again, I saw hope operating in a variety of people in the same ways. To enable people to use this pattern as a helping tool, I named it, quantified it, and taught it in workshops: *The Hope System*. By recognizing each person's hope system, I could connect with the dying where they really live.

But first I had to understand where I really lived, what really moved and motivated me at the core. I had to unearth my own hope system, just as in this book readers will be asked to do, before being able to walk with the dying on their final journey.

I started out my life's work tending to the dying, which has turned out to be my true calling, getting the best education possible at that time for this type of work by joining a convent. The religious community that I entered at age seventeen was a rather unusual one for the time, the late 1950s, and it was this difference from other teaching orders of nuns that attracted me. This congregation was called Nursing Sisters of the Sick Poor, which described its mission: the care of the sick poor in their own homes. The Sisters seemed to be more compassionate and kind to the people and patients with whom they worked. They were freer than other medical professionals and assisted and communicated with people in a very real and special way that appealed to me.

In 1961, I was sent forth to become a nurse. I came into nursing in a way that is now almost extinct, through a diploma school of nursing that combined intense class work with working on the units actually caring for patients. In effect, nursing students staffed the hospital, working all three shifts—days, evenings, and nights. For various reasons (mostly as punishment for some infraction or another), I seemed to always be working the night shift, but that turned out to be a gift. It is a well-known fact that most people die at night, usually between 2 A.M. and 4 A.M. So it was from the dying themselves that I learned my most valuable lessons early on.

Although I was just twenty-one and only a student nurse, I always had a sense of comfort with the dying, and I was never anxious or afraid of the experience in any way. Well, my hands never shook, anyway, but you never saw my knees—because of the habit. I realize now that it was a preparation for the rest of my life.

In the early 1960s we were still in the old full habit, with only our face visible (for "custody of the eyes") and dressed completely in white from head to toe when we worked in the hospital. Many patients, especially the dying, would call us angels and our very presence seemed to calm them as death came near. Because we were Sisters, they thought we had an inside track on helping people as they came to the end of their lives.

When we were sent out to care for people in their homes, we were not allowed to receive gifts, of course, and neither could we take anything with us except a sandwich and a tea bag. I remember the first day after graduating as a nurse—July 7, 1964. As part of the Nursing Sisters of the Sick Poor, I was dropped off at the subway station in Jamaica, Queens, to begin making my rounds. There I was in my full black habit (a nun's street wear), a rather medieval sight in gabardine—cincture (belt) gripping my waist as if girding me before battle—my nursing bag, along with my sandwich and tea bag in hand, when my long rosary caught in the subway door! Good thing I was young and could run to keep up with the train, and that the rosary was on an elastic cord with a Velcro closure.

We took a sandwich and a tea bag for our lunch, because the only thing we could take from the poor was water. There was tremendous freedom in being able to care for patients in such a pure way, asking nothing from them, requiring nothing from them but the privilege and opportunity to care for them at life's end. I now realize that it was this freedom to be able to be with patients and their families in such an extraordinary way that kept me in religious life for so long.

I did home nursing for the majority of the sixteen years I was a nun. This time afforded me the opportunity to accompany literally hundreds of dying persons on their final journey. We would take care of them during the day, return to the convent to say our prayers, eat dinner, and often go back out and stay with them throughout the night until they died, caring for them and supporting the family.

In subsequent years, I have worked pretty much nonstop with the terminally ill and their caregivers and grieving families, primarily in home care and in all types of institutions—hospitals, hospices, nursing homes—performing jobs on all levels, including managerial positions and as director of nursing. Concurrently, beginning early in my career, I developed workshops on grief and The Hope System for both professionals and laypeople, learning much, in turn, from the 40,000 students I've taught throughout the United States, Canada, and in Europe. My work has been recognized as pioneering the improvement of end-of-life care and I am frequently sought out to describe it, on television, the radio, and through other media outlets.

Beginning in the early 1970s, I also participated in the beginning of Therapeutic Touch, with Dolores Krieger, Ph.D., R.N., and Dora Kunz, the science-based healing art that is used in more hospitals in the United States than any other complementary therapy or form of energy work. I also teach it, and developed a technique based on its principals, which many people feel comfortable employing with the dying, called The Hand-Heart Connection (see Chapter 9).

My early life choices, and all those that have followed in the last forty years, gave me the opportunity to become the ultimate companion many times, placing me on the receiving end of the gift of insight. There have been so many journeys, each made in his or her own way, yet each and every person so generous in sharing their wisdom. We have much to learn from the dying. It is my privilege to share what they have taught me.

Facing death may be life's most difficult challenge, an inner journey. But, in this book, as a I did when a member of the Nursing Sisters of the Sick Poor, I use a gentle way of moving readers through the process of dying, increasing their awareness of life and living as much as of the process of death and dying.

I believe this book is timely enough to meet the needs of the babyboomer generation, and it can be seen as the helpmate that helpmates have been waiting for: a systematic guidebook for how to navigate this voyage into the unknown, by conquering fear with compassion.

Offering practical advice in a way readers will be able to use, regardless of their beliefs, The Hope System addresses all levels of the experience—physical, emotional, psychological, and spiritual—within the embrace of that thing called "hope," just as the dying do. Hope is the foundation of the dying person's world. By systematically learning how to recognize and honor a dying person's hopes, anyone can support him or her from first diagnosis to last breath in a way that is healing for all.

What is hope? Hope is many things, with as many responses as there are people to whom one asks the question. Hope is like a diamond, being multifaceted; often clear and sparkling, sometimes a bit cloudy with a hint of yellow; or perhaps it appears dull and lifeless.

- Death of the person closest to me
- Parts of my body or my life most difficult for me to lose
- My own death

Write down the first words or phrases that come to mind under each of these columns. Don't worry about spelling or grammar, just write.

Have an internal dialog about your responses. Mentally walk in the footsteps of the terminally ill, exploring your feelings as you do so. If you take a minute to do this exercise before reading on, it will allow you to compare what you write with what others have written without being influenced by what they wrote. Each of us have our own unique way to respond to these questions. There are no right or wrong responses; each response is "normal" for you. By doing this exercise you will learn from the "laboratory of the self" some of what the dying may experience from the moment of the life-changing diagnosis to the moment of death, as well as your own feelings about death and the dying.

Five Columns Workshops

I have tested this approach with thousands of workshop students—health-care professionals, laypeople, and the dying themselves.

As my workshops begin, I ask participants to turn off their cell phones and consciously let go of all the busyness, responsibilities, and demands of their lives and to take an inward journey with me.

Column One

We start with the life column. Underneath that word I ask that they write whatever "falls out of their mind onto the paper." I tell them not to worry about spelling or grammar, but to just let the words flow onto the paper, inspired by the word *Life*.

When they have finished writing, I ask them to call out words from their individual columns, which I write on a white board to make a composite column for the group to see and reflect upon.

The responses from the life column usually flow easily and sometimes I have to slow the participants down in order to get all the answers on the board. For the most part the responses are light, easily shared, and quickly fill the column. Frequently the patterns that emerge have to do with daily life, work responsibility, relationships, love, joy, family, and children. Faith and God come in. Words and phrases that are recurrent in this column include *beach, water, trees, hiking, picnics, taking walks, the color green, blue skies, sunsets, sunrises,* and *vacations.* Difficult subjects such as *money, not enough time, too much work, loss,* and *death* usually don't come up until the end of the column.

We talk for a few minutes about what these terms mean to us. At this juncture I start using the phrase *normal and unique* to describe for them their particular response to this word *Life.* I explain that each response is unique to them and their personal life experiences, and, if they are caring for a dying person, unique to the bond between that person and themselves. Each response is normal as well, in that it is normal for them to feel as they do. Guilt and self-recrimination should be left at the door.

At the end of our discussion, I ask that they count the number of responses in their life column. Their entries often exceed twenty. Subsequent columns usually have considerably fewer.

As you read this, have you been able to see similar words and patterns in your own response? Do you think your responses are normal? Can you see how they would be unique to you and your particular life experiences?

Column Two

At the top of the next column I ask students to write the word *Death* and to again write their responses. When the group has finished writing, I ask, "Is there a change in the room? Has something happened here?"

Often I sense my asking these questions brings a feeling of relief. I hear sighs and comments such as, "It *is* darker now." The terms *heavy, sad,* and *quieter* often come up. Some people express that they feel uncomfortable or that they felt a pall come over the group.

The students are always interested, as you may be, about a phenomenon I have repeatedly observed with this *Death* column. It is my experience that people's handwriting changes somewhat when writing in this column. People are often surprised to find they have written their responses smaller, bigger, printed instead of using cursive, or different in another way when compared to their life column.

In order to help the participants go deeper into themselves I ask the question, "If there was not such a noticeable change in atmosphere in a group of health and hospice caregivers, should I be concerned? Why might that happen?"

Some of the answers heard most frequently are: "They are in denial" and "They have become hardened or burned out."

In addition to the above, I usually add that the health caregivers may not have personally experienced death, so it is not real to them. It is not part of their consciousness.

I then discuss a common, unexplored motivation—often existing on an unconscious level—that I have found to exist in groups of people drawn to work with the dying. They may have experienced the death of someone close to them at an early age (birth to toddler) or at a developmentally fragile time, such as when they were a teenager, and it has left a deep imprint on them; a mark that has not been uncovered or dealt with in their life thus far. Many people recognize this in themselves for the first time during my workshops, as others share similar early death, loss, and separation experiences they have endured.

I also have observed that the entries in the *Life* and *Death* columns often contain similar responses regarding the "grounders" or stabilizers inherent in peoples' lives. These include family, friends, and other support people, and transcendent elements, such as faith, God, and a belief in an afterlife.

Column Three

When we are done discussing this column I write: "Death of the person closest to me" at the top of the third column on the white board. As I do this, I often begin to feel a change in the room. When I finish writing, I turn in anticipation of their question. I say, "It may be someone who has died or someone who is still alive, whatever comes to your mind first, just go with it, and let the words flow out onto your paper."

As I wait for them to write in their own column, I frequently observe behaviors different than I did when assigning the first two columns. There are more tears and expressions of sadness and discomfort in the group. Many people sit and stare, cross their arms and glare at me, or look away. Some begin writing furiously, while others need to go to the restroom or leave the room for awhile.

I sense when the group has had enough time and begin the dialog by asking, "What happened here?"

Some of the responses I have heard repeatedly are:

"You brought it all back."

"Awful."

"I refuse."

"Everything went black."

"Tears and sadness."

"I'll never get over it."

Others are:

"I was surprised by who came up as the closest."

"It was hard to choose who was the closest; I had more than one."

"I remembered what she was to me."

"I lost the love of my life."

"Memories are a great gift."

I can feel their eyes on me as I record on the white board the generally heavy emotions felt and expressed quickly and clearly by the group. I push them a bit, sharing that, "I feel another strong emotion, that none of you have mentioned. What do you think it is?"

Silence usually prevails so I answer my own question: "I feel anger, strong anger, mostly aimed at me." At this moment I again stress that all their feelings are normal and unique to their life experiences and the relationship they had with the people who died. "Why wouldn't you feel angry?" I ask. "How dare I make you think about this and feel this way?" They often say something like, "Boy, Cathy, you have a lot of nerve," or, "Yes, why?" Again I stress the importance of lessons learned in the laboratory of the self.

Perhaps you had similar feelings and responses as you wrote under column three.

My next question to the group is, "Was there anyone who was not able to write in this column?" Usually there is at least one. "Was everyone able to choose someone who was the closest to them? How many of you could not respond or write initially? You needed to wait, push the paper away, but then after awhile were able to respond?"

I tell them that those who reacted in this manner demonstrated in a profound way what people are going through when they are faced with the possibility of the death of the person closest to them. It is a common first response to deny the likelihood of death, push it away, run from it, because it is too painful to even consider that the person they love and need, by whom they are defined in so many ways, will die and leave them.

Next I ask how many of the students put a relationship such as mother, father, or spouse at the top of the column. (My personal definition of closest, which is the presence of both a love bond and a need bond in defining the relationship, is a concept further explored in Chapter 6.)

Many respond in the affirmative and a dialog ensues. Then I ask if anyone wrote a name at the top of their column. Rarely in my workshops, does someone do this. For the most part students say something like, "It makes it too real if I put a name." Another response is, "I wouldn't put his name down because then it might happen, or come true. I don't want to jinx anyone I love."

I ask how many of the class thought about someone who had already died. I ask how long ago. The answers range widely, from a few months to thirty years. Then I ask, "How did writing about it feel to you?" The answers may be:

"It felt like yesterday."

"I saw her face again."

"It helped to remember."

"You made me miss her again."

"I can't believe it's been twenty years."

I use their responses to bring out another gift of this column, that even though time has passed since a death, the memory of it can bring on brand-new feelings. This demonstrates that grief has no timetable and that lingering or latent negative feelings from the past can be reexamined and reconciled in the present. This may be done by talking it over with someone or saying things previously left unsaid in a letter to the deceased or in a journal. Other rituals of remembrance and release may be employed as well. Catholics often have masses said for loved ones who have died.

All of this demonstrates that the grief process is often quite difficult and prolonged. It may require outside help and assistance to cope with it and live on.

In my experience, denial and anger are the two strongest feelings in response to this column. So, why do I do it? Why do I push my students? Because I am asking them to explore and understand what they themselves are experiencing. This helps them to understand not only themselves, but, in their role as caregivers, it helps them understand what those closest to the dying go through.

This is a good time to break and have refreshments, and to walk about. Often students will come up and share more with me at this time. If someone has had an intense and emotional response and has left the room, either I seek them out, or if they have come with someone, I send their companion to find them. I ask if I am needed to intervene; if more time is needed.

I then continue and students return when they feel ready. It is interesting to note that among the thousands of people who have come through my workshops, I have only had one woman who was not able to return. She realized that it was too soon after her mother's death to attend something as intense as my presentation.

Column Four

At the top of the next column, I ask the students to write, "Parts of my body or my life most difficult for me to lose." I encourage them to choose parts of their body first and then they can choose any other aspect of life that comes to mind.

Again, I sense a change in the room's atmosphere. Initially it is lighter, then it seems to darken a bit. My first question when students have finished writing is to ask how many chose a part of their body. Most hands pop up. When I ask, what they chose, "My eyesight" is always the most frequent response. This is followed by loss of hearing, mobility, independence, hands, legs, and almost universally, loss of mind.

As I continue to talk with the group I will hear the words *breast* and *uterus* come forth, usually expressed in a tentative voice. If I do not hear or see any of these personal responses, I suggest them. What comes out is the deeply hidden fear that loss of the parts that define one as a man or woman is just too scary to verbalize or put into words. In all my years of doing these workshops, only once did a man mention prostrate in the group setting, and never was the word *penis* spoken.

As I mentioned earlier, the change in atmosphere is again different for this column. People respond slower and more thoughtfully. When questioned about their responses, I get comments such as, "I thought column three was the worst, but this surprised me in its intensity and was harder than I thought it would be," and, "It came too close; it was not someone else." Many relate that it is difficult for them to make such choices.

The primary theme that emerges is that losing a part of oneself is actually perceived as a "little death." Suddenly, one is vulnerable to death itself.

Following this, interesting dialog begins and I hear sighs of relief as the group shares things other than their body that would be most difficult for them to lose. *Children, spouse, partner, companion,* and *lover* usually top the list. *Faith, independence, energy, God, the ability to love and be loved, a sense of humor,* and *the ability to think* frequently appear. *Joy, hope,* and *nature* are also mentioned regularly.

These responses flood out of participants' mouths, and column four begins to overflow, a virtual inventory of the most important things for them to hold onto, those attributes which, on many levels, mean the value of life itself, not just survival.

One important result of this column is that it helps participants understand more deeply why the dying often became very pensive or quiet prior to death. They are mourning the past loss of parts of themselves and preparing to lose all they have known.

What were your responses? Did you write similar words or expressions as the groups had or did you write something different? Remember do not judge. Yours and their answers are normal and unique. There are no wrong answers.

Column Five

Usually I ask the group what they think column five will be. Suggestions pop out and finally I hear, "Our own death." So, on the top of the fifth column, I ask students to write "My own death." To make it more personal and revealing, I tell them to imagine how they want to die. Where? Alone? If not, with whom?

Almost universally I hear:

"No pain. I cannot bear too much."

"I want to be alert and pain-free."

"Finish my business."

"Say good-byes."

"Make amends."

"Be right with God."

"See loved ones again."

Since there are always many who mention pain I ask, "How many of you want your death to be quick and painless?"

Many respond affirmatively. Then I hear:

"Not too fast or sudden."

"I want enough time to say good-bye"

"...time to finish my business."

"Not too much time! I don't want to suffer."

"I don't want to have my death prolonged."

"I want to live, not just survive."

"Not yet, I'm not ready."

The absence of pain on the physical level is the highest priority in all my workshops, followed by absence of pain on emotional, mental, and spiritual levels. Quality of life issues come to the fore in this column. What is universally shared is that the absence of pain on many levels is what brings about a peaceful death.

I push the class to write everything they want for their death in this column.

"I want a party."

"Please celebrate my life."

"No tears."

"Leave with a job well-done."

"I want to die after seeing my children's children, until the fourth generation."

"I don't want to be put in the ground. Cremation is the best."

"Bury me in my pink dress."

"No wake or funeral."

As you can imagine I've heard practically every kind of way to die imaginable.

"I want white satin sheets."

"Out under the stars."

"Surrounded by family."

"In the arms of my husband."

"Cryogenics for me."

"In my sleep."

"No machines, just let me go—let nature take its course."

"At home."

"Not in the hospital."

When we have filled this column to overflowing with their wants, I encourage the students to go home and share their thoughts with their loved ones so their wishes may be honored. It never ceases to amaze me how many people, even among caregivers to the dying, do not have wills or other pre-death and post-death arrangements made for their families.

In summary I ask the group, "Why did I ask you to do this on this lovely warm day?"

I may hear:

"To help us understand what both the dying and their families go through, to resensitize us, to help us 'feel.'"

"To learn what to hold onto and what to let go of."

"What is really important to me in both life and death?"

"Dying is not an easy process."

"How to be there with family and patient because I walked in their footsteps here today."

I tell the students that all of their responses are right on, but ask them to go a little deeper into themselves and ask what they saw when comparing their own column with the group's column. They answer that they had very similar responses as the group's.

I explain that I have done this exercise with groups across the United States and internationally. I have done it with preschool kids with leukemia using finger paints for their columns; with school-age kids using drawings, clay, and oral stories; with teenagers using their favorite songs; with adults stricken with cancer and AIDS; and with the families and friends of all these people. "If I place their five columns on top of your five columns, what would we see?"

Students answer:

"The same responses."

"Similar words or expressions."

"Even without words, their pictures would tell the same story."

Then I ask what this means to them. And I hear:

"We are all the same."

"We are all connected."

"Working with the dying is learned by experience, not from books."

"The dying have all the answers if we listen and ask the right questions."

Finally I ask, "What have you learned and experienced today? What do you think is the greatest gift we have to give the dying?"

Responses are:

"Compassion."

"Listen, look, and learn."

"Greater understanding of what they may be experiencing."

"We are all normal and unique."

"The dying are our greatest teachers."

I close by telling the class that the greatest gift we have to share with the dying person and those who love them is our humanity, as death is part of life; the two are intermingled realities, each with its own perspective.

If our humanity is the most important gift we have to share with the dying, how do we, who are so much a part of the living, share this gift with those who are on their last journey as a living person?

Let's build upon some of the lessons of the Five Columns exercise:

- That death is a part of life.
- That we too will die.
- That we all have a fear of death.

These general principles—the three assumptions underlying my clinical approach to dying persons and their loved ones—can become your own touchstone in your effort to be present for the dying. Having looked inward to deepen awareness of your own feelings about death, you are now prepared to look beyond yourself, to better understand the needs and behaviors of those actually confronting death.

This is also the first step in exercising true compassion. And compassion, as distinguished from sympathy, and, even empathy, is the engine that drives the healing gift of humanity from one person to another.

Three Parts of the Fear of Death

We learn to become a listening presence (how to *be there* when it counts) first by listening to self (through the Five Columns exercise), and next, by learning to *hear* what the dying fear in death. The follow-

11

ing examples from my own experience with the dying demonstrate how to discern which of the three parts of the fear of death a person may be focused on. Is it:

- fear of the process,
- fear of the moment of death, or
- fear of the hereafter?

By knowing what the dying fear in death, we can intervene more realistically and help them to have a death that is peaceful. I have found that asking a patient, "What do you fear in death?" is definitely *not* the way to elicit this information. And, for the most part, we don't need to use such a direct approach. What I have learned over the years is if we listen carefully to a person's words and actions, we hear and see what they most fear.

Fear of the Process

As an example of the fear of the process, my patient Joe, at first, appeared to be focused on his treatment. Then I began to hear a change in him: "Cathy, my aunt died of cancer and what I remember about it was that she suffered a lot." Clearly, Joe "told" me that his prevalent fear was fear of the process: "Will it be painful? You don't have too much pain with my problem, do you, Cathy?"

Armed with this knowledge, the care team knew they must really help him manage his pain and provide relief for his symptoms during every step of his journey to a peaceful death. "What I remember is that she really suffered. I hope this medicine keeps working like the Energizer Bunny," Joe said.

Fear of the Moment

Fear of the moment of death is expressed in a variety of ways. I have seen patients turn day into night, sleeping all day and lying awake all night. Still others want the lights left on and need reassurance that "someone will be here all night." For those with this fear, we need to have family members or other caregivers stay with them at night to decrease their fear. Darkness and death often become synonymous in the mind of the dying as they feel their end coming closer.

"Death comes like a thief in the night." "He slipped away in the middle of the night." These thoughts aren't totally irrational; as I mentioned, most patients die between 2 A.M. and 4 A.M.

Leaving lights on, playing the radio or TV, bringing the patient out to the nurse's station, moving him nearer to where people and activity are, along with administering mild antianxiety medications, palliation (pain relief/comfort care), and the listening presence of another all help to dispel the fear of the moment when life meets death.

We may do all the above to help the dying have a peaceful passage, but as we will learn in Chapter 6, the choice of the when, how, where, and with whom the patient chooses to die, is always up to them, as it will be our choice when our time comes.

Fear of the Hereafter

From my expereince, fear of the hereafter, manifested as a fear of the unknown or of possible judgment, is the third most prevalent fear the dying have. Frequently this fear is raised in a most interesting way. I've been asked the question: "You've been with a lot of people who have died, haven't you, Cathy?" After I answer in the affirmative, they query, "Do you think there is anything after death? Where do you think we go after…? Do you believe in heaven or hell? What if I can't forgive someone?" I share my thoughts and beliefs with them and ask if they need to speak to someone more "in that business" than I am. Often they do, but are reluctant to come right out and ask.

I have found that the fear of judgment and the need for reconciliation on the spiritual level increases as death nears.

At this point the caregiver's mediator or messenger role comes into play. Patients have said, "I haven't seen my brother in over twenty years. We had a fight and I don't even remember what we fought about." Many times their spouse or kids are angry as well. Here, I ask the question, "How may I help you?" knowing that their statement is a plea for help to come to peace and/or reconciliation in this matter. Then I or another team member, pastoral care or social worker, will make the call or write the letter to get this person's message to the loved one, thus providing help in "mending fences." Being able to reconcile with family or others can decrease the fear of judgment after death and decrease the physical, mental, emotional, and spiritual pain prior to death.

13

Listening and hearing what the dying fear most in death enables us to help them achieve the peaceful death they are hoping for.

What are You Hoping for?

As you read this, you may wonder how I came to this way of relating to both the dying person and their loved ones. The answer is quite simple: The dying themselves have been my teachers in the forty years I have been assisting them. They taught me how to enter their private world. How did I get them to teach me? Simply by asking them the question, "What are you hoping for?" and then allowing their answers to guide me in *how to be there* with them on their final journey.

John

In particular, one patient of mine illustrates how effective this question can be in facilitating understanding and communication between everyone involved: patient, family, and professional caregivers alike.

Years ago, as part of my role as a clinical nurse specialist in oncology, I was asked by the staff of a medical oncology unit to see a man named John. They said that he seemed a bit down, and maybe needed someone to talk to. A former policeman, he was a perfect example of the strong, silent type, but the staff had sensed sadness in him recently. In my visit with him, we got to know each other some. He spoke openly about his diagnosis and prognosis, and lovingly about his wife of fifty years and his family.

During our conversation I asked him, "What are you hoping for?" He replied quickly, "I hope the Mets win." So we both smiled and exchanged baseball stories. After chatting a bit more, I told him I would return to see him again and then I left, understanding from his response that John did not want to explore anything more deeply with me at that time. This simple question drew John out of his medically defined role of the compliant patient, and gave him the opportunity to regain his sense of self as the full person he was before his diagnosis, not simply as a cancer patient.

Several days later, as I was walking down the hall, I heard my name called, and turned to see John walking toward me with his ever-present IV pole. He was accompanied by four men, each one taller and bigger than he. These were his four sons: two policemen, a fireman, and a detective.

"Cathy, I want to talk to you," John said. "Remember the question you asked me the other day? I want you to ask me it again."

By this time, John and his giant sons had surrounded me—I felt like a small sapling gazing up at giant redwoods—and I responded dutifully, "I asked your father what he was hoping for."

Looking directly at me, John gave his real answer: "I hope my sons will understand that I don't want any more chemotherapy. I want to go home and be with their mother and see my grandchildren, without vomiting my guts out, for as long as I have left to be with them."

The sons looked at him and then at me and I can assure you there was not a dry eye among us.

John went home that very day. He spent quality time with his wife, his children, and his grandchildren, just as he hoped he would. And then he died peacefully at home, his wife and his sons beside him, assisted by a local hospice team.

Perhaps the most important lesson that John taught me early on in my career, one that has remained and grows stronger to this day, is to always remember how difficult it is for families to let go of their loved ones, and how much of a struggle it is for the patient to leave those he loves as well. But in patient-centered care, it's the person who is ill who has the final say in how he lives or dies.

Being asked, "What are you hoping for?" brought John back to his personhood, because the ability to have hope is the core of the self—the essence of what it is to be human. As long as you're alive, you have hope. And sometimes hope is the only grasp you have on being true to yourself. Reconnecting with his own personal hope system empowered John to change the course of his life. He could then decide how he would live out his death. He could derive the peace that comes from making the choices that reflected his deeper hopes for himself and his family.

As a result, John was able to live and die as he hoped he would. In addition, his sons would live on after his death knowing that they truly listened to their father and chose to honor and respect his wishes as he was dying, just as they had done in life.

As I mentioned, I like to give people tools that are simple and that work. As you can see from John's story, learning about and showing simple consideration for what a person is hoping for is great at cutting through the patient-role limitations to return an individual to full personhood in their own eyes and in the eyes of everyone who is relating to them.

Realizing the power of this simple, yet profound, question has changed the quality and effectiveness of my interactions with dying persons and their loved ones ever since I met John. I know it will help you, as it has helped me and many others, to accompany the dying in a fully human manner.

The Power of Hope

Here I would like to introduce the concept of "the power of hope." Hope is an interior force, a powerful, usually conscious, but sometimes unconscious, motivator.

Hope existed before we were born in the utterances and desires (hope systems) of our parents and grandparents:

"I hope it's a boy to carry on the name."

"I hope it's a girl after three boys!"

"I don't care as long as the baby is healthy."

Hope is a current flowing through life, guiding and directing us, changing in strength as we need it. It stretches from the mundane to crises large and small:

"I hope to ride my two wheeler without the training wheels by my birthday."

"I hope I get on the little league team."

"Mom's sick; I hope she doesn't die."

"I hope I get my license."

"I hope I get invited to the prom."

"I hope to become an architect."

"To graduate summa cum laude is my hope."

"I sure hope she says yes!"

And of course the hope of every beauty queen: "I hope for world peace!"

Hope is such an integral part of our lives that, like breath, we could not live without it. And, like our breath, hope adapts to the many changes and crises we face in life, and provides us with the internal strength to cope with and live through even the most devastating, life-threatening situations. Hope is the belief that potentials may be fulfilled. And, just as hope is apparent throughout our lives, it is never more apparent than when we are staring death in the face.

Since hope is an energy manifestation of the human essence, it is useful as a therapeutic modality. Hope is an integrator of all life's processes, the interweaving thread that binds those processes together, making a cohesive design, creating a unique pattern that becomes the hope system of each individual. Hope alters or affects our perceptions, enabling us to be open and increasing our realm of possibilities.

We are confronted with the power of hope as an internal motivation force. Let us consider the wellspring of hope, rising from within the person, empowering the person to behave in ways that achieve self-fulfillment. Hope facilitates the true development of the potential of each human. (It is only in death that our full potential is realized.)

The power of hope is a premise on which The Hope System was developed and the ensuing chapters are based. The Hope System emphasizes how much of an advocate within us hope truly is. This can't be emphasized enough, because traditionally the concept of hope has been relegated to the sidelines, like an unreasonably avid, blindly-optimistic fan.

Too often we use phrases like, "hoping against hope," or "hopelessly unrealistic," to describe a positive attitude that flies in the face of negative odds, whereas, for a person face-to-face with death, hope functions as the most genuine guide of all. In my experience of observing and communicating with the dying, the role that hope serves in the transitional process could almost be described as that of a hormone. Indeed, the most current research on hope is in the biological sciences, as if hope were a part of our endocrine system, possibly no less vital than other hormones.

Jerome Groopman, M.D., in his book *The Anatomy of Hope*, writes, "Researchers are learning that a change in mind-set has the power to alter neurochemistry. Belief and expectations—the key elements of hope—can block pain by releasing the brain's endorphins and enkephalins, mimicking the effects of morphine. In some cases, hope can also have important effects on fundamental physiological processes like respiration, circulation, and motor function."

A remarkable insight is that *the basic needs of the dying are also those of the living.* The three basic needs of the dying are:

- The need to know they will not be abandoned,
- The need for self-expression, and
- The need for hope.

Through examples in the following chapters you will learn ways in which hope itself gives us a rationale for feeling hopeful when nothing else does. Even when circumstances seem to give us no grounds for hope, the act of hoping itself establishes its own rationality. Recognizing the power of hope is important for several reasons:

- In acknowledging hope as a positive force, caregivers strengthen the dying person's strongest inner advocate, which promotes healing.
- In listening without judgment, caregivers support fulfillment of the dying person's second basic need: the need for self-expression.
- From birth to death, hope enables us to shape and reshape our concept of self-identity so that we can thrive in alien territory, even against the seemingly insurmountable odds of terminal illness.
- Hope is an integral part of the life-death process; it is the mechanism by which we gain access to the reservoir of our own (and the universal) intrinsic life force.
- In accepting the expressed hopes of the dying, caregivers support the quality of life for the dying, which often enables them to outlive their prognosis.

The hope system within each of us is that from which we draw the strength to face and deal with life's challenges and struggles; the courage to face change, from birth to death, with equanimity. This is apparent throughout our lives, but it is all-pervasive as we proceed on our journey toward death, the final stage of human growth.

In this chapter, you've examined your own attitudes toward death and have gained an understanding that, in general, the basic needs of the dying are also those of the living. With this accumulated awareness of how alike we all are, while still acknowledging the importance of respecting individual differences, you are ready to focus on what distinguishes those facing imminent death from the rest of us, as we'll do in the next chapter, "The Four Stages of Hope."

Chapter 2

The Four Stages of Hope

Elisabeth Kübler-Ross, a renowned psychiatrist—and also my teacher when I began my work with the dying—brought into the medically dominated, cure-oriented world of the 1970s, a new framework of thinking about the dying. She insisted that families, friends, and professional caregivers must all acknowledge what the terminally ill were going through psychologically. And, in its time, this was indeed revolutionary. But she, as well as I, always sensed that there was something more going on than psychology, something deeper—but we were not able to name it then.

The Five Stages of Grief

Kübler-Ross attempted to give patients some kind of control over their fate by helping them understand the psychodynamic shifts they were going through. By classifying these shifts—naming them "the five stages of grief"—she identified the psychological behaviors of the dying person and the coping mechanisms they used from diagnosis through death.

Her first stage is *Denial*: "No, no not me."

Then *Anger* comes in: "Why me?"

Anger is followed by the *Bargaining* stage: "Yes me, but..."

The next stage is *Depression*: "Oh my God, I'm going to die."

And the final stage is *Acceptance*: "I'm going to die, and somehow it's all right."

What Kübler-Ross did was identify behaviors and coping mechanisms. And this was a monumental advance in its time. By itself, it sparked a revolution in how we all think about the process of death—and a revolution in how the medical profession treated the dying.

But both Kübler-Ross and I realized that, revolutionary as her five stages were for that time, they were only a start. Why did we think that? We felt that way because the psychodynamics of this scheme reflected *only a part* of the dying person's experience. As time went on, her five stages turned into a set of rigid boxes, with people artificially trying to move the dying from one stage to another ("Okay, let's move him out of his denial now.").

Doing this in such a rigid manner carries with it the danger of reducing the dying person to some fragment of his whole self. As I mentioned, this was much more common than you'd want to believe—doctors or nurses talking about "the cancer in Room 30" or "the heart attack at the end of the hall." Again we were restoring the old impersonal, purely clinical habit of viewing the dying person as nothing more than their medical or psychological status.

I realized that we needed to view the patient *as a whole person*, rather than as a disease or as being at a certain psychological stage in the dying process.

Taking up where Kübler-Ross left off, and with her blessing to take the next step beyond her approach, I developed a unique framework for understanding the dying person and responding to what they are *experiencing internally as a whole human being*. My approach, which I introduce in this chapter, expands and deepens Kübler-Ross's stages, which are solely from a psychodynamic perspective. It keeps the patient's family and the caregivers focused on the dying patient as a whole person, fully present on all levels—physical, emotional, mental, and spiritual. And when we relate to the dying person in this way, we are being a fully-aware person ourselves, rather than the unaware, fearful person so many of us become around a dying person.

The Hope System

I named my approach "The Hope System"—which prompted Kübler-Ross to call me "The Hope Lady." My approach enables the caregiver and the family to understand that *the dying person's hopes are central to his or her wholeness, and must be respected fully*—rather than reducing the person to a reflection of the psychological stage they are going through at the moment. Thus, The Hope System goes well beyond both Kübler-Ross's psychodynamic approach and the medical model, by bringing back the concept of the whole person as the focus of how we think about and relate to the dying patient.

The four stages of hope are:

- *Hope for Cure:* "I'm gonna beat this thing!"
- *Hope for Treatment*: "I hope I'm in the 29 percent that chemo helps!"
- *Hope for Prolongation of Life*: "I hope to walk my daughter down the aisle."
- *Hope for a Peaceful Death*: "I hope I die pain-free and alert."

These four stages of hope alert the caregiver and the family to what is going on in the inner world of the dying person, as their hopes change in the face of impending death.

In this book, I provide you with practical, time-tested tips for how to relate to the dying patient as a whole person. You will learn new ways of *being with* those who are dying, ways that are effective in meeting their needs. I will show you why, when we put the concept of hope and The Hope System at the center of how we relate to the dying, we are not just honoring the whole person in the dying individual, but are also honoring the whole person in ourselves. After all, if we fall into the trap of reducing the dying to nothing more than a disease, a diagnosis, or a stage in a psychological framework, we are also failing to honor our own wholeness as a person.

The Dignity of the Dying

My approach is intended to restore the dignity that has so often been lost due to the "medicalization" of death—the twentieth-century trend of people no longer dying at home but rather dying in an impersonal, cold hospital room at the end of the hall. The Hope System helps family and professional caregiver alike to recreate how people were routinely treated when they died at home, as fully human until their last moment—and never as merely "the cancer in Room 32."

In addition, as we honor the dying in this humane manner, we learn to assist them on their final journey. Guiding them in this manner teaches us how to live our own lives more fully each day.

It is crucial to realize that when we support a patient's hopes in this manner, we meet the three basic inner needs of the dying, as mentioned in Chapter 1:

- the need to not feel abandoned,
- the need for self-expression, and
- the need for hope.

Four Journeys

Now at this juncture, I invite you to walk with me in the footsteps of four of my most memorable patients as they make the four stages of hope come alive. As I share their stories it will become apparent that from diagnosis until death there is continuous movement back and forth, between and among the four types of hope.

Martha

First, let's meet Martha, the wife and caregiver of a hospice patient of mine, living in a fifth floor walk-up tenement apartment building in a South Bronx neighborhood. On one of my visits, she had shared with me that she noticed "something" in her breast in the shower, and she asked me to look at it. I immediately encouraged her to see her physician, who upon examination sent her to a surgeon for evaluation.

Listen with me now as she tells me what she heard the doctor say: "When I went to the doctor about the lump in my breast, he said, he could cut it out and then everything would be all right." Her words clearly tell us that her predominant hope is hope for cure.

We may never know what the doctor actually said to Martha, but what she heard was very much determined by what she was hoping for in regard to her condition.

Another important fact in her hope for cure was that her husband was terminally ill, and he needed her to be cured so she could take care of him. In fact, she refused postoperative chemotherapy and radiation and is fine to this day, still living in the same neighborhood and taking care of her grandchildren.

Charlie

Our second story takes us to Long Island and the radiation therapy department of a large hospital. In my role as a clinical nurse specialist in oncology, I sat in on all the initial interviews with the radiologists, to discuss the treatment plan with each new patient. In one such interview, I was drawn from the first moment to a big, loud, tough teddy bear of a man named Charlie. Charlie had the thickest Brooklyn accent I'd ever heard—and being Brooklyn-born myself, I'd certainly heard many people who spoke "Brooklynese."

One afternoon when I returned from lunch, I literally bumped into Charlie as he exited the treatment room. Greeting me with a big smile and booming voice, he pointed at his large protruding abdomen, swollen from a big tumor, and said, "See this tumor, Cathy? Between me and the cobalt, it doesn't have a chance!" We were attempting to shrink the large tumor so that surgery could be performed to remove it.

There were many strikes against Charlie: He was obese, he was a heavy smoker and drinker, and he'd already had heart surgery for a triple bypass. However, armed with the power stemming from his predominant hope for treatment, "me and the cobalt" and his underlying hope for cure, "it doesn't have a chance," Charlie's response to treatment was amazing in view of his type of tumor and his medical problems. As a matter of fact, we were actually able to shrink the tumor so that almost all of it could be removed, and he outlived his initial prognosis of three to six months by living two and one-half comfortable years—until his heart disease took its toll on him.

Jane

Next, come with me to sunny California where Jane and her husband are still reeling from the news they heard that morning at the doctor's office: "There is nothing more we can do for you, Jane," their doctor had said.

"When he mentioned hospice, we wanted to know what to expect—does that mean I have to be dead in six months?" Jane asked. After I assured her that she didn't have to die within six months to come into hospice, she said, "Oh, I'm so relieved to hear that! You see, my daughter is two months pregnant and I hope to be here for the birth and be able to hold my first grandchild." Jane's husband and I heard her words of hope loud and clear: Her predominant hope was hope for prolongation of life, since she knew there was no more treatment for her.

And her hope for prolongation of life was not simply about how long she would live, it was about the quality of the life she would lead during that time. She felt that by coming into the hospice now, we would help her control the symptoms when her condition worsened, and help her remain comfortable so that she could be at the birth and be able to hold her grandchild "even for a little while." With the help of the hospice team—and empowered by her own hope system—Jane was able to be there at the birth and hold her grandson. Indeed, she almost made it to his first Christmas, outliving the one to three month estimate the doctor had written on the original referral for hospice care.

Frank

Crossing the country, let's return to the East Coast and visit Frank, a gentleman I had the privilege to accompany for several years on his journey with head and neck cancer. Like his disease process, Frank's journey took many twists and turns, as did his almost continually changing hope system. This was due to the many and various treatments he tried that he hoped would lead to a cure. Frank had endured radical surgery twice to remove the original tumor that had spread to his tongue, then experimental chemotherapy and, finally, a long course of radiation therapy.

I have chosen to share Frank's story with you not just because I knew him for such a long time, but because he taught me so much about the importance of listening to, and trusting, the inner wisdom that I have found is so strong within people with an incurable disease. Walking with him, we traveled from hope for cure, to hope for treatment, and back again a number of times—with hope for prolongation of life popping up to enable him to live through all the treatments he had successfully endured. My companions on Frank's journeys of hope hither and yonder were his wonderful wife and children.

After Frank's last surgery and his discharge, I received a note from his wife telling me that he had been able to go see his mother, finish his business with her, and finally tell her he loved her and said good-bye face-to-face, which brought him the peace and reconciliation he had hoped for since childhood.

Several months passed, and one day I received the phone call that I had been, both waiting for and dreading: I heard the head nurse on the medical floor, not the surgical floor, say, "Hi, Cathy, Frank's back and he's asking for you." This time I knew what to expect and I also knew we were both hoping for the same thing. As I entered the room, Frank's blue eyes twinkled and his warm smile greeted me. Then slowly I saw how thin and weak his body had become. As his wife came to greet me and we held each other, I saw the tears in her eyes. Frank handed me his ever-present yellow pad on which he had written so many changing hopes over the years, then he took my free hand and held it tight, looking me straight in the eye as I read what he had written. "Cathy. Do you think the medicine will keep me comfortable until…?"

"Yes, Frank, we will keep you comfortable until…" I answered, with our eyes still locked in place. He smiled his thanks for my reassuring words. Over the next three days, I witnessed his hope for a peaceful death become stronger and stronger until he died peacefully in the arms of his loving wife. He had left me one more message on the yellow pad before he died. It read: "Cathy, I hope you can continue to be there for my wife. Thanks for everything. Frank." I still have all of Frank's messages written on those yellow pads. Each time we move, my husband holds them up and I say, "Put them back in my special box; I don't care how ragged they are, they are still precious to me."

These stories illustrate how The Hope System connects us to the humanity of the dying. This tool enables both professional caregivers, as well as the patients' loved ones, to constantly relate to and connect with the dying person as a whole person.

What I have learned over the years is that there is a special "body wisdom"—almost instinctual in nature—that is triggered in those with a terminal illness, as the disease progresses within them. Thus, each stage of The Hope System is activated by the progressive physiological changes caused by the terminal illness itself, and each provides an opportunity for the caregiver to seek out the needs that are specific to the individual at that moment, in order to understand what to do or say or not do or say.

James

For example, when my patient James felt that his treatment was doing nothing but causing more pain and weakness, he stopped saying "I hope this treatment works," and asked me, "If I stop radiation now, will I be able to walk or sit in a wheelchair by June?" If all treatments have been exhausted, this question becomes the cue for the most helpful response, which is not blurting out, "You can't stop radiation now!" but rather asking a question: "How is that month significant for you?" or "What's happening in June?" The answer might be, "My daughter's graduation."

The caregiver's next question, "What are you hoping for?" might be answered with "I'd like to be able to see my daughter graduate."

In this scenario, James is telling us that his hope system has shifted from hope for treatment to hope for prolongation of life. That stage of hope usually indicates that a person has accepted that medical treatment cannot affect a cure and that now he or she is hoping for medical intervention that promotes quality of life for the time they have left, such as an adjustment in their pain medication.

This latter stage of hope can be difficult for a loved one to accept; yet it's important to acknowledge what is heard and alert the medical staff to this change. (Chapters 7 and 8 provide practical advice on how family members and health-care professionals can best handle such scenarios.)

Patient-Driven Care Through Listening

The ideal, based on all my work with the dying, is for long-term care and end-of-life care to be *patient-driven*. There is a wisdom in the dying that drives the transitional process from within—a wisdom that they first feel, and then express, *in their hopes*.

Once caregivers and loved ones *really listen to* and acknowledge where the patient is in their hope system, they often find that:

- We activate great reserves of strength even in the most physically incapacitated patient.
- We bring them great relief and open the door to further and deeper communication.

- Talking with patients about their hopes makes it easier for
    the caregiver to understand what the dying person needs.
- Being in sync with the patient's hope system allows the
    patient and loved ones more quality time together, for
    mending fences, expressing love, and for all those things
    that provide the best chance for a peaceful death.
- Caregivers and loved ones are prepared for a healthier
    grieving process, one without remorse or regret,
    knowing they have treated the dying patient as a
    person, not just as a diagnosis or a disease entity.
- There is no such thing as a person without some type of
    hope—no one can live or die, for even a moment,
    without hope.

If we acknowledge that, at a core level, the patient himself is hope itself, we can see why hope is where we need to center our expectations, both as family members and professional caregivers. As the terminal illness progresses, hope actually comes closer to the surface than ever before. When a person is presented with a terminal diagnosis, hope begins to rise from the inner depths, on call now, on guard, our corporeal sentinel and guide. Spend one day with someone recently diagnosed with a terminal illness and you will understand the power of hope.

The Hope System helps the patient, the caregivers, and the families in two different ways. First, it is a tool that immediately reveals what's happening within the dying; second, it helps us learn what they need from us, based on their expressed hopes, and tells us what we need to do. Through its four stages, The Hope System provides a model that anyone can use to support the person's predominant hope at each moment on the deepest level, as they care for him. Understanding the four stages of hope alerts the caregiver to what's going on in the patient, as his primary hope stage changes in the face of impending death.

Being Present

As I've learned from the journeys of my patients, very few of the dying move through the four stages of The Hope System in a predictable and orderly fashion from stage one to stage four. During such an intense time, their hopes change in more of a back-and-forth zigzagging pattern than a linear continuum. But the patient and their family may be experiencing different fluctuations and be out of sync with each other.

The most important lesson of all is that when you acknowledge whatever stage of hope the dying person is currently going through, you are being there for them when it counts; you are serving as a listening presence.

By learning to track which stage of The Hope System the dying person is going through over time—what their specific hopes are and how they are changing—you become able to engage with them on the deepest level, on a continuing and ongoing basis. In becoming aware of the changing hopes of the dying patient, and resonating with these hopes, we avoid the trap of projecting our own hope system onto them. We actually hear what it is *they* are hoping for, instead of hearing what *we* imagine they are hoping for, or what we think they should be hoping for.

Making such a meaningful human connection—by asking the one simple question, "What are you hoping for?"—is healthy for all concerned. It is sure to foster clearer communication, a vital factor in ensuring appropriate medical treatment and patient-directed care from the moment of diagnosis all the way to the moment of death.

That this approach should be as effective as I've found it to be in thousands of patients and their families isn't all that difficult to understand: After all, we are what we hope—the dying as well as the living. And, as we learned earlier in this chapter, our own humanity and wholeness are enlarged by asking this critical question, and listening to the answer. By acknowledging *their* hopes at every stage, we are more in touch with our *own* hopes, both before and after our loved one or our patient has died—and are more fully able, as survivors, to live our own lives without regret or guilt.

Chapter 3

The Patient's Journey

No matter how we define this somewhat mysterious and fascinating four-letter word, we probably agree that *hope* is not passive; it has an intrinsic energy within it that seems to direct, guide, move, and change people through their life situations. Never is this dynamic force more apparent than when one is confronted with the reality that one's own life is limited and will, in a certain matter of time, come to an end, that moment when we face our own death.

Having been involved with dying persons and their families in an intense way for the past forty years, I have become acutely aware of this deep, intrinsic force within each human being, and have studied it at great length. The cornerstone of my own approach to dying persons and their families begins with the following sentence, which introduces the inner world in each of us where hope lives and moves and waits to be addressed:

> *All of us can live with the knowledge that we have an*
> *incurable disease, but none of us can live with the thought that we*
> *are hopeless.*

Let us examine this phrase that plays such a key role in describing what follows. The patient's acknowledgment of having an incurable disease, "something fatal, which will ultimately take my life," occurs first on the intellectual level. Then, in time, this knowledge of incurability slowly filters through the mental, emotional, physical, and spiritual levels and certainly has a deep effect. Faced with this devastating knowledge, this person can still live out and complete life. One knows it is possible to live even with the slow progression of disease robbing vitality until death arrives.

Hope Is Essential

None of us can exist in this world with the thought of hopelessness, for hope is an integral part of all levels and aspects of each individual. Could you live with the essential condemnation of you as a person, of your very essence, who you really are? Being labeled hopeless is like being declared a non-being, an object, not a human being, with all that entails—no history, no present, no future—truly a death sentence far more devastating and destructive than the disease that may be spreading unmercifully throughout your body.

We humans, when devoid of our hopes, feel robbed of the essence that defines us on all levels.

Surely none of us would want to be thought of as "Room 308—just a hopeless case." This type of insensitive statement demonstrates a somewhat prevalent attitude still among some health-care providers today: "Since there is nothing I can do for the patients, since I am not able to cure them of their diseases, why stay involved with them at all?" Thus, the abandonment of the dying subtly begins.

People need to die as they live, with their intrinsic life force, their individual hope system, in place. If we want to relate to the dying as human beings, we must not deal with them as hopeless cases, but rather direct our energies to accompanying them on their final journey. In order to do this, we must be willing to help them unearth their own hope systems.

Everyone's hope system can enable them to live each day until they die as the whole person they want to be, no matter what the depth or extent of the physical disease they are enduring. Despite all their suffering on a physical or emotional level, hope opens for them the possibility of realizing their full human potential. Indeed, the crisis of impending death can create tremendous opportunities for growth in many dimensions of who we are as humans.

It is deep interior hopes that enable the dying to live each day in the face of incurable disease, until they are ready and able to let go and face death.

The Hope System approach to the dying reaches into and relates to each person's intrinsic hopes, for we are what we hope. In order to understand the key concept of The Hope System, it is necessary to emphasize that hope, our interior life force, is merely changing. It is never destroyed. Hope is always present with each person experiencing the final life-into-death passage, and it motivates each one to live through the dying process from the moment of the fatal disease or condition's diagnosis, until death.

Imaginary Journey

In order to present The Hope System in a more real and meaningful way, I ask you to take an imaginary journey with me—the same journey that all patients take from the moment they are diagnosed with a fatal disease until they confront death. Here the four tenets of The Hope System are: Hope for cure; hope for treatment; hope for prolongation of life; and hope for a peaceful death are presented as the actual dying person may experience them.

Let us pretend that you have not been feeling well, simply not yourself, more fatigued than usual, without any specific reason you can attribute to this change. Perhaps you might have noticed a small swelling in the glands of your neck or underarm, or a lump that does not go away, or a persistent cough, or painless bleeding.

You, like all patients before you, go to the doctor and he validates that indeed you are looking a little tired and pale. He wants to take some blood, or upon examining the swelling states that he will biopsy that enlarged gland or lump. What would you, as every person before you, hope for at that moment? Some responses from actual patients have been, "Please let the blood work show only a strep throat, mononucleosis, or even hepatitis, but *don't* let it be leukemia or any kind of cancer or AIDS. Whatever the diagnosis is, please let me have something that can be cured!" Thus, you arrive at the first step of The Hope System, which is hope for cure.

Let us continue on our imaginary journey. The doctor, upon receiving your blood work, says, "I don't like the looks of this report. I'd like to put you in the hospital for more tests." Perhaps, after reviewing the test results, he states, "I'll have to cut that out, but I'm sure I can get it all. Perhaps you may need some radiation to the area, but after that everything will be okay." While we are still primarily hoping for a cure, another factor has been introduced, i.e. various treatments to effect a cure. We now put our hope into the treatment modalities to bring a cure. Thus, the second stage of The Hope System comes into being, hope for treatment.

The Hope for Treatment

The hope for treatment phase is the focusing of hope as a life force, or empowerment, into the treatments. This strengthens the patients, enabling them to endure the pain and discomfort created by modern curative approaches such as chemotherapy, disfiguring surgery, radiation therapy, or experimental medications and protocols. The strength or power of our hope system is apparent throughout this period, and it becomes a driving force that empowers us to get through the treatment. This interior source, which I call the power of hope, enables most patients to withstand not only the application of their therapies, but the side effects that are often more uncomfortable and debilitating than the treatments.

The hope for cure and hope for treatment stages are often quite prolonged, due to the variety and intensity of treatment approaches that our modern-day technology has produced. In addition, within this phase the cure may have many faces and wear different hats. Cure may mean hoping for temporary cessation of the spread of cancer or hope to control symptoms or bothersome side effects of experimental protocols as is often the case with people with AIDS or other chronic terminal illnesses.

There are variations in the intensity of individual hope systems noted during this time, no matter its length, depending on the effectiveness of a treatment modality at any given time. For example, shrinking a tumor through the use of radiation or chemotherapy for a certain period of time may bring relief. Utilizing radiation therapy to control or decrease bone pain, thereby increasing comfort, movement, and function may definitely affect both the intensity and duration of hope within this phase.

Changes in the intensity and length of The Hope System may also stem from the medical world's ability to effectively control the side effects from disease progression or the treatment modalities themselves. Health providers now have a large variety of medications and alternative or complementary approaches to control nausea, vomiting, and diarrhea. Steroids and nonsteroidal anti-inflammatory drugs are also useful to reduce inflammation or swelling, thereby controlling nerve and bone pain.

The time period marked by hope for cure and hope for treatment varies with each individual, and depends on all the factors of disease progression, available therapies, and the patient's response to treatment modalities, plus the various side effects caused by treatment approaches. Medications or treatments with possible cure potential, such as protease inhibitors in the cocktail for persons with AIDS, also directly affect the length of time of both these phases of The Hope System.

All these combined factors, as well as the emotional, psychological, and social interplays within and external to the patient at any given time, contribute to variations with the patient's hope system. Each factor appears to play a role in igniting an inner reality, or interior knowing, moving a person from within—from a primary hope for cure to a more specific hope for treatment that will effect a cure at this time.

However long or short this time sequence is, it does come to an end. It is put on hold or pushed into the background. This shift in hope is triggered when at some point in time, the medical world says to the patient and family, "There is nothing more that we can do for you. We have exhausted our armamentarium of treatment approaches for your disease," or, "Surgery is no longer an option for you now." They may state, "At this time, chemotherapy would be ineffective," or make a similar comment.

The Hope for Prolongation of Life

The patient's individual hope system is quite unique at this time, and the patient often responds in a most remarkable way when confronted with this information. These words speak of death, since those whom we saw as having the power to save us are no longer able to do so. Rather than being totally crushed by this life-threatening message, almost immediately an amazing change takes effect. Our intrinsic life force is actually enlivened, not destroyed, by these statements. The ill seem to be able to reach down into their inner core of hope and summon up the strength they need to live out their lives for as long as they hope to live. I call this stage hope for prolongation of life.

There are myriad manifestations of the hope for prolongation of life in the many levels within the terminally ill, each expressed in distinct ways. Some will state that they hope for a miracle. Others say that they hope for time, because "In time, if I live long enough, they will find the cure and miraculously, I will be saved; that is, I will be cured."

Kübler-Ross' stage of bargaining is frequently heard within this phase of The Hope System. Bargaining enables both patient and family to acknowledge the reality of the possibility of death, but it also brings in hope to hold death at a safe distance. Frequently they say, "I want to see my daughter graduate," or "I want to be able to hold my grandchild." Obviously one has to be alive to both see and hold. So, while the major hope is no longer for cure or treatment, it is certainly for life, not just for survival.

It is in this phase that the quality-of-life issues become paramount. During this stage, the importance of the control of pain and symptoms that are robbing patients of the quality of their remaining time must be dealt with effectively, competently, and compassionately so that their hopes are respected and affirmed.

Some might say that hope for prolongation of life is synonymous with the will to live. However one may choose to define this very real time period, I have been amazed over and over again by the strength and tenacity seen in the dying at this time. For example, I have seen patients who have agreed with their physicians to stop IV and tube feedings, who are unable to eat or drink, and live not only for days, but weeks. In fact, one patient (who you will read about in Chapter 5) lived on literally nothing for weeks in a comatose state, unable to discern night from day or mark the passage of time. Defying all the rules, he lived until his birthday so that his wife would be able to receive his Social Security and pension benefits.

Perhaps in your own life you have experienced a loved one or a patient "hanging onto life by a thread." Frequently we see the dying wait for their favorite child or special nurse to be with them at the moment of death. I have seen patients hold on or wait until after a major holiday like Thanksgiving, Christmas, or a birthday so that time of happiness and celebration is not marred by their death.

The power of this phase enables many people to outlive their prognoses. The capacity to hope for and experience life to the fullest does determine the individual's ability to participate fully and knowingly to achieve his or her highest potential. It is the difference between truly being alive and living fully, and just surviving. It has to do with the quality of life, not just the fact of life or simply existing. The hope for prolongation of life means, "I choose to live fully alive in the face of a terminal illness and hope that I am given the control I need to live out my life in the manner I choose."

The Hope for a Peaceful Death

When the fundamental hope is no longer for cure, treatment, or prolongation of life, there are significant behaviors that indicate that the primary hope is for a peaceful death. These are so significant that they are discussed in detail in Chapter 4. These behaviors are all indicative of the person shifting his focus from the things of life and all that life has meant to centering on his own death. Becoming quiet, withdrawn, refusing to eat or take medications—all life affirming behaviors—to actually turning their backs on the world and the significant people in their primary worlds are all indicators of the fourth and final stage, the hope for a peaceful death.

As we examine this hope, we note that the hope is not simply for death but death that is peaceful. The important question is, "What makes death peaceful?" Peaceful means the absence of pain, first and essentially, on the physical level, because the presence of physical pain distorts both life and death and becomes a barrier to the peace we are hoping for at life's end.

Secondly, the emotional pain of strained or shattered relationships prevents peace from entering the patient's life at this time. This, to me, is the most excruciating of all, the pain of mental anguish caused by the lack of completion or closure in our human relationships.

Lastly, attaining peace on the spiritual level is exceedingly important as life comes to an end, since forgiveness and reconciliation with the divine, however experienced, appear to be necessary components in many people for peaceful death to become a reality.

Hope for a peaceful death possesses its own intrinsic power. Once your primary hope is for death, this hope actually empowers you to let go of life and become focused on death. This major shift from holding on, to releasing life, changes one's demeanor, attitude, and behaviors, allowing death to become more and more real. In fact, it becomes more real than life itself. The dying become preoccupied with the reality of death, as life and all that life symbolizes loses importance and no longer holds the dying's attention or life energy. At this point, death often comes quickly to the patient who is now open for it. Many appear to let go with resignation; others are resigned initially, then as their interior dynamic reality is tapped, they are filled with the serenity of acceptance, as their hope for peaceful death becomes reality.

There are, however, as we all realize, those who never come to peaceful death because they cling so tenaciously to life or loved ones that peach in death cannot find them. These are the people who die "kicking and screaming," who do not go "peacefully into that dark night," those who fight to the bitter end.

The Progression

By respecting a person's expressed hopes, we support the patient where he really lives and nourish the vitality intrinsic to the moment he is in. By allowing him to experience each stage of hope at his own pace, we maximize the potential of his own interior energy to organize and guide him at a speed he can handle in the way his hope system knows best. In the previous chapter we learned that though these stages exist on a continuum in theory, in people they commingle, and a patient can go from one to another stage of hope and back again in the flash of an eye. This is a good thing because it allows the inner dynamism of hope its full reach, but it can be a confusing thing for those of us on the outside looking in.

When I was the first person to be licensed by New York State as a clinical nurse specialist in oncology and thanatology in 1975, I was only just beginning to learn how elegantly these various stages of hope can coexist—and work for—a patient. They spiral back upon one another to gain power, giving the last stage its much-needed energy, almost like a pitcher's windup before the final throw.

Perhaps a real life clinical example will make four stages of The Hope System come alive for you.

Frank

Frank, the patient of mine we met in Chapter 2, had been readmitted to the head and neck surgery service and he requested that I come to see him. Frank had five prior admissions in two and one-half years, and, when last discharged, he had a permanent tracheotomy and feeding tube. That visit, for all intents and purposes, had been considered his final visit. At that time, we had sent him home to fulfill his hope, to enjoy spring in his garden. My predominant hope based on previous experience with Frank during his prior hospitalizations was hope for a peaceful death. Frank had been through so much and, in my mind, had suffered enough. Herein lies the danger of clinical thinking.

To my surprise, an elated, animated, though weakened man, greeted me. In a lively manner, communicating by using penciled notations on a pad of yellow paper, he began to describe a new surgery the doctor was going to try that perhaps would enable him to be rid of the feeding tube at last. He then left for the radiology department, giving me time to reflect and reexamine my own feelings. In order to be effective in this or any therapeutic trust relationship, it was necessary for me to be clear on my own hope system, which was affected by my knowledge, intuition, diagnosis, clinical experience and, of course, my personal feelings for the patient.

First, I had to be clear about what I had hoped for Frank. In all honesty, I was still hoping for a peaceful death for him. But, what was his predominant hope? Certainly, hope for treatment predominated, with underlying hope for cure, and, at the least, hope for prolongation of life. He wanted to have the surgery, be rid of the tube, and go home again.

Second, I had to avoid imposing my hope for a peaceful death on a person whose hope system had returned to hope for treatment. The support, information, and understanding that this patient required to support and strengthen his own hopes at this time differed greatly from the attention he would have needed had his predominant hope moved to the peaceful death phase.

Yet, I soon realized that Frank did not fit nicely into one stage anymore. His years of endurance under the gun had seasoned his hope system into something like the solar system. All the stages of hope he'd been through were now interconnected, revolving around each other, harmoniously, it seemed. He was hoping to have the surgery, be rid of the tube and go home again. For him, now, a new hope for cure was supported by hope for treatment with hope for a prolongation of life a steady hum underneath it all. How could I impose my hope for a peaceful death on a person whose hope system was revving for life?

Whether or not my hopes for him also shifted at this realization was immaterial. My behavior had to shift into line with the patient's hopes, not with my own and not necessarily with those of family members or loved ones. None of us had cancer of the head and neck except for him. So I had to release my thought that he had suffered enough and go where he and his wife needed me to be.

In addition to this, I was assigned several other roles to support his needs and hopes—again written on sheaves of yellow paper. These written hopes and needs were clearly his reality. First, he asked me to find out from the doctor exactly what the surgery entailed and then explain it to him and his wife. He also asked me to continue to be there for his wife.

How clearly he had written out his hope for prolongation of life with hope for treatment and ultimately hope for cure, using these words: "For me, life is to be able to go home without this feeding tube!"

How necessary it is for caregivers to hear the predominate hopes of our patients so that we may more realistically accompany them on their individual journeys.

I consciously adjusted to being the swing person, moving from my comfortable hope for a peaceful death to wherever he and his wife needed me to be to make his clearly-expressed hopes become reality.

I then set about coming in early to meet with his surgeon. This truly tested my own ability to support his primary hopes. I did not like his doctor and my clinical mind questioned how he could do this surgery. It included a special graft to the affected area, which I was not sure contained enough viable tissue due to the previous extensive surgeries and radiation. Would the graft take? After explaining the surgical procedure, I felt compelled to share my misgivings with Frank because I cared about him and took seriously the trust he and his wife placed in me. They both smiled knowingly as I spoke and were relieved by my honesty. Having shared my concerns about the surgery, I then was able to commit myself to being there for them and supporting them in their hopes, not my hopes. This I did with the totality of my personal and professional being.

Frank did have the surgery and, despite the odds, he came through the procedure beautifully. He also healed, even with all the damage from radiation therapy. The feeding tube was removed and he went home.

Without the embarrassment of the feeding tube, he was able to travel to Florida to see his aged mother in a nursing home and to say good-bye to her. His hope for cure enabled him to finish this important business. He lived almost another year with a high quality of life.

At his last admission to the hospital, he wrote on those same yellow pages, "Cathy, do you think the medicine can keep me comfortable until...," and, "Cathy, I hope you can continue to be there for my wife." This time I knew we were both at the same place and that the predominate hope was indeed for a death that was peaceful.

Again, both husband and wife requested my presence, but this time it was not for information but for palliation, comfort, and care. Frank did die peacefully in the arms of his loving wife. As a team of three, we enabled his hopes to come true. He accepted and understood the hope for peaceful death as the final stage of his life.

Using the metaphor of a patient's hope system being like a solar system, while you are within its reach (as you are in the role of caregiver), you are just another planet following universal laws. It is his world, it is his reality, that counts. If hope for cure pops up again after going home to die peacefully, so be it. Frank's hope for cure enabled him to have a final visit with his mother, which won him a feeling of satisfaction that, in turn, helped him live for almost another year in relative comfort.

The clinical application of The Hope System has proven effective by providing a language and guide to better understand and communicate with dying persons and their families. I feel it is crucial for all of us interacting with the dying because it enables us to get to the heart of the matter. That is, it helps us clarify what the patient is hoping for from his experience, his treatment, his surgery, his hospitalization. Thus, it helps us understand what both life and death mean to this individual in each step of his journey from initial diagnosis until life's end.

Chapter 4

How the Dying Speak to Us

The symbolic verbal and nonverbal languages of the dying are known as "separation behaviors" and are triggered primarily by the physiological changes that occur within the terminally ill person as the disease progresses. The behaviors that we see are the external manifestation of their inner world, that world within which is known only to them. It is part of the body wisdom, which alerts them to the changes that signal their demise. This mind-body interaction is given to them so that they may prepare for their own death and the resultant external, observable words, and behaviors are the language that they use to prepare those whom they love.

Thus, the interpretation of this special language is of prime importance for all those who would accompany the dying on their final journey. It has been my privilege to be taught this language by the best teachers, the dying themselves. It is now my privilege to share this with those of you who desire to learn it and wish to hear and understand the dying's final messages.

The Language of the Dying

I want to explain some of the words and behaviors I have observed so that when you see or hear one or two, or perhaps more, in a given situation with family or a patient, something will click. You will not only see and hear but understand what the dying are truly saying, and be able to interpret their language and symbols to help prepare yourself, no matter what role you have.

You, then, will be able to assist others who have a relationship with the dying person prepare themselves so the death is not as traumatic or devastating as it might have been without this knowledge and help.

I have never seen all of the following behaviors occur in one person. Yet, I have seen similar themes repeated time after time. These patterns emerged in the hundreds of dying persons I have accompanied on their final journeys. The behaviors and words are the language of the dying.

Between Depression and Acceptance

If one chooses to use the stages defined by psychiatrist Elisabeth Kübler-Ross in her book, *On Death and Dying*, to describe the dying process, a review of her work is helpful:

- The first stage is *Denial*: "No, not me."
- Then *Anger*: "Why me?"
- The third stage, *Bargaining*, is: "Yes, me, but..."
- The fourth stage is *Depression*: "Oh my God, I'm going to die."
- And the fifth is *Acceptance:* "I'm going to die, and somehow that's all right."

The time period I wish to discuss now occurs around the fourth stage as the person is moving toward the fifth stage. This period of resignation may be characterized as: "Yes me, and no more buts."

It is important that we clearly understand that the length of this time period is different for each person experiencing it and unique to their individual life-into-death transition. For example, over the years I have seen people in which several of the nonverbal behaviors occur in one day and then suddenly this person dies after having been on hospice care for several months. I have also observed nonverbal and verbal behaviors occur over months.

All of the symbolic verbal and nonverbal behaviors that follow are anecdotal evidence of the dynamic reality of hope within each of us. Our hope system comes to the surface, becoming real and observable when we face the crisis of our own death and all the things that mean life are being taken from us. When we are stripped to our core, we come in touch with our true-life force, wherein is our ability to hope.

We can observe all of this in others. As the disease progresses, it is like layers of an onion peeling away. The roles of work, family, and responsibilities that have constituted the person's life drop from importance. Now that the external life raiments have been stripped away, a deep inner dynamic—hope—is freed and comes to the foreground. It comes up to consciousness now because its power is needed so that the dying person may live each day the way he hopes to live it until he dies. This deep inner connection with self is what keeps one alive. It stems from the same deep reservoir within that all human beings share, and becomes activated when life is threatened.

Inner Sustenance

An aspect of The Hope System that has come to me over the years of observing the life-into-death process of so many people is that there seems be a shift in attention from "outer" to "inner" sustenance within each individual's unique way of letting go of life in order to grasp the reality of their death. The phases of The Hope System and the separation behaviors that follow capture and describe how this process takes place. Hope begins their journey, hope sees them through it, and hope brings them to its culmination in death.

For clarity, I have divided the symbolic language into two categories—nonverbal and verbal. I shall begin by describing the passive nonverbal behaviors, which form a significant part of the separation behaviors utilized by the dying to prepare themselves and their loved ones for their death. It is my hope that as you read on you will be able to see or hear more clearly, and now perhaps understand, the communications so lovingly delivered to you by those who have gone before you in death. You will also see that death is not a passive process, but a process that possesses within it a tremendous dynamism.

Passive Nonverbal 1

Behavior: They stop eating, drinking, and taking medicine.

Interpretation: They stop doing all the things that mean life and socialization and begin to disconnect from life and loved ones. They may also be taking charge of their life and death by choosing these actions.

Action: Don't force them to eat, drink, or take medication. Dehydration is a normal and natural part of the dying process. Their bodies are shutting down, and they don't require the nutrition and hydration they did in the past. It is important to adjust the method of pain and symptom control as the patients change to insure their comfort.

Passive Nonverbal 2

Behavior: Their eye contact changes. Initially, the dying look deeply into the eyes of loved ones, absorbing each feature. Over time their gaze shifts. They seem to be looking through us, beyond us, as if we were no longer there. They look to the left (heart side) or up to the ceiling as if looking at someone or something behind us.

Interpretation: Their change in gaze and focus indicates movement from those who are in their life toward their death. This often-subtle shift symbolizes the disconnection or letting go of physical life and loved ones. Often they begin seeing loved ones who have died or other spiritual beings at this time.

Action: Don't question this. Try to understand the subtle but powerful message contained in this behavior. They are now able to see beyond us, to see where they are going. Their life is no longer with us. They don't see themselves with us here any longer, but are now able to see the reality beyond this world. They now seem to be more "there" than they are "here."

Passive Nonverbal 3

Behavior: They pretend to sleep.

Interpretation: They are closing their eyes on the world and life and us. The things and people of this world are no longer important to them. The eyes are our windows on the world, and they are shutting theirs. They need to withdraw into self, to begin their inward journey.

Action: Allow them to rest. Do not try to wake them up or engage them in conversation. Explain this behavior to family as, "Sleep in preparation for death." It is not a rejection of loved ones.

Passive Nonverbal 4

Behavior: They request that we close the blinds or curtains on the window.

Interpretation: They are closing out the light of the outside world. They no longer wish to participate in life outside. They are retreating into their own world, which is necessary for their transition and signals the life-into-death process.

Action: Darken the room for them; don't argue with them. Respect their wishes. They need to close out the outside world and distractions. Focusing on the outer world is not as important now as inner-world focus is.

Passive Nonverbal 5

Behavior: They ask that the curtain between them and their roommate be pulled closed.

Interpretation: They are blocking out others, stopping communication and participation in life and community. They need time and quiet to focus within.

Action: Do as they ask. They need their energy directed inward. They need privacy to connect with their inner self, so they can finish their business. Inner communication is now more important than outer communication.

Passive Nonverbal 6

Behavior: They display changes in visage, from furrowed brow, facial grimacing, or a look of distress. Over time facial expressions change and relax. They appear calmer and more peaceful.

Interpretation: Physical relaxation response indicates the struggle of holding on is ending: "He's not with us anymore." "It feels like she's drifting away." Reality of death is present and with it comes resignation and relief.

Action: Observe and learn from this behavior. Do not hold onto them. Let them go. Give them your blessing and permission. This may be their final gift to you: "She looked so peaceful at the end. No more suffering."

Passive Nonverbal 7

Behavior: They become quiet and withdrawn, no longer talking.

Interpretation: By not communicating with loved ones, they are further withdrawing into self, not wanting to be part of the world or life. Interior communication is the most important task at this time.

Action: Respect and understand these important changes. This behavior is difficult for all caregivers, as we want to do something. In this behavior, the dying are trying to teach us the importance of being rather than doing, a crucial life-death lesson. In sharing the silence and just being present, we create a safe place for the dying to complete their journey. You might say, "I know you don't want to talk anymore. But, may I just come and be with you?"

Passive Nonverbal 8

Behavior: They turn their back on visitors.

Interpretation: They are turning their back on life, the world, and us. Their life energy is now more and more involved in their personal inner journey than the things and people in this world.

Action: Don't say, "Turn over; look at me," or interfere with this behavior. Allow and understand it, not as a blatant physical rejection, but rather with knowing that they are, with love, preparing us for a life without their presence. The deeper meaning to this is, as they turn away from us, they are turning toward their death. They are no longer part of us or our world. Silently, they ask us not to hold onto them, but let them go to their death. This is a powerful cross-cultural theme.

Passive Nonverbal 9

Behavior: They go into the fetal position.

Interpretation: They are turning physically inward. This movement signals that the dying are now, on all levels of their being, more and more involved in their inner journey. They are intensely preparing for their transition and delivery from life into death.

Action: This is an extremely powerful separation behavior. Analogy and symbology of this behavior is necessary for death as it is necessary for birth. Both can be seen as transition from one life into another. It is not only symbolic, but it is a necessary component of the life-into-death process. That's why it's so difficult for people who are tied down in ICUs or a nursing home to die, as they are not able to go into fetal position and complete their transition. We must allow the dying to die in their most natural way.

Active Nonverbal 1

Behavior: They physically push away those close to them, not allowing them to care for them anymore. They push caregivers' hands away if they try to feed or medicate them.

Interpretation: After having attempted the passive nonverbal behaviors and turning away without success, the dying now need to do something more active and direct to get their message across. They are symbolically pushing us away from them and death into a life without them. This communication is used by the dying as a last act of love.

Action: While you or the family may feel rejected, don't get upset or angry or feel the person doesn't love you anymore. The dying person feels frustrated. This is not done in anger but rather because they love us. They are trying to prepare us for, and spare us from, the moment of death. They are pushing us to understand and to let them go.

Active Nonverbal 2

Behavior: They move the arms back and forth from the center of the body to the sides. This movement usually occurs with fists clenched, as if breaking out of a shell. I have also seen pushing with open hands, as if moving through a web or cocoon, trying to get out.

Interpretation: They are breaking out of the physical shell which has encased them in life. The dying have a powerful need to free the spirit or life force. They are attempting to free themselves from their physical confines and pass into a new dimension of being. This behavior may intensify as death comes closer, but cease as the actual moment of death nears and their struggle is over.

Action: Do not attempt to stop or restrain them. However, it is important to protect them from harm. Understand and appreciate their silent words and hear the message this graphically signals, "It's my time to leave here and be freed from disease, pain, suffering, and life itself." It also demonstrates how difficult it is to leave, to let go of what was known as life. But this is crucial in order to die.

Symbolic Verbal 1

Behavior: They verbally push people away. The dying frequently use anger or language they never used in life. Family members are surprised and apologetic. "He doesn't mean it." "It must be the medication." "I never, ever heard him use words like that."

Interpretation: The dying often use anger or shocking words to get their loved one's attention. This is employed when all passive behaviors have failed to get the message across and their loved ones are still holding onto them.

Action: Don't react with anger or stop them. Rather, listen to their pleas, hidden within the anger or foul language: "Please listen. Hear my message. I'm dying. Release me. Let me go." The dying are vehemently requesting that their loved ones give them permission to die at this time.

Symbolic Verbal 2

Behavior: They ask loved ones and others working with them to leave. "Mommy, go home. Jimmy needs you more than I do now." "Nurse, I'll be okay. Go over there, that woman is crying; she needs you."

Interpretation: They are sending loved ones into a life without them. This is especially dramatic when seen with children who often send parents home and, no sooner than the parents leave, the child dies.

Action: By stating the needs of others before theirs, they are symbolically releasing loved ones to re-engage with others or their life without them. This gives family members the opening to say, "I hear you. I'll go on without you. Do what you need to do. I'm not alone; I have what I need."

Symbolic Verbal 3

Behavior: They use illogical travel metaphors or analogies. "Hurry, we must find Henry. He has the plane ready to take me." "I have to go. I don't want to miss my train." "I don't want the bus to leave without me. The tickets are in my purse."

Interpretation: Many use travel analogies to indicate movement toward death. These are symbolic assurances to the family that it's time to leave. They are used to calm loved ones. The dying are telling them they have a way of getting there; they are going home; that others know the way and will take them to their destination.

Action: Listen intently to their message. Don't hesitate to ask questions about people and mode of travel: "Where is the bus going?" "Was Henry a pilot?" The dying want loved ones to know that others know the way, have the means to take them, and that they are not going alone. It's important to tell them that you understand and that it's okay for them to leave.

Symbolic Verbal 4

Behavior: They speak to and see those who have gone before and/or religious figures that bring peace to them. "My mother came to me last night. She smiled at me." "God is there, waiting for me with open arms." "The angels came to get me one: big one and two small ones." "I saw my brother." "They're all there waiting for me, just across the river."

Interpretation: They are symbolically telling those close to them that "It is my time." They are ready, and they can, and must, go to see and be with spiritual beings and those who have gone before them. The dying "see," and now know for certain, that others are waiting for them and are able to help them come to them and find the peace and presence they have been longing for.

Action: Encourage them. Don't negate what they say. Ask them questions: "Tell me about them." "How many angels have come to you?" They are symbolically telling us where they are in the dying process. They are giving us assurances that others are there to help them cross over. "I will be with the others who have gone before and are at peace." "No more suffering." "You can let me go now." "I'll be just fine. I'm not alone and I'm going to a better place."

Reactive Depression

Many of these behaviors, such as the cessation of talking and eating, withdrawal and isolation, if seen in any other population would be called depression. In the dying population this pre-death phase is called "reactive depression." They are reacting to what is happening in their body and an increasing awareness of their impending death. This depression, like dehydration, is a normal part of the dying process and it is very important for the dying and for us. To help us understand this behavior I have divided it into two parts—anticipatory and preparatory.

Anticipatory

It is anticipatory for the dying person, who, on a deep and profound level, is anticipating his own death, thus the going inward. He may seem far away now, withdrawing into himself, completely absorbed with doing his interior work. "He's not really here with us anymore." "I can't reach her now; she seems so far away." "He's more there than he is here."

Preparatory

It is preparatory for the family and caregivers alike. The dying are trying to prepare us for their death by dismissing us from their life. "You don't need to come and see me anymore." "I'll be saying good-bye now." Frequently, I have heard them say to a spouse of many years, "Only come and see me once a day (or skip tomorrow). It's too long a bus ride." These statements have nothing to do with how long the bus ride is, but rather have everything to do with the deep awareness of the reality and proximity of their death and the need to prepare the other for it.

Since this reactive depression is part of a very important process, I recommend the individually-determined and judicious use of antidepressants for the dying. Antidepressants should be given only to take the edge off the depression and thus assist the dying in doing their work. They should *not* be given because this depression makes the doctor, family, or professional caregiver uncomfortable. Depression is an essential and normal part of the final journey and should not be interrupted. We must always remember it is not about us or our comfort; it is their dying, not ours. I've had patients say to me, "Cathy, please take that pill away; I can't do my work; it's hard for me to focus on what's important since they gave me that new medicine."

Final Words

The verbal and nonverbal cues contained in the symbolic language of the dying are an attempt to prepare those closest to them for their death and a life without them here on earth. They desperately want to ease the trauma for their loved ones in every way possible. These separation behaviors are triggered by the physical changes they are feeling as the disease progresses and they become aware from the inside out that they really are going to die, and they become aware of *when* they are going to die. Thus, they seek the right words to help their loved ones hear their final messages, prepare for living without them, and to be able to let them go.

Chapter 5

The Hope for a Peaceful Death

As we observed in previous chapters, the last stage of hope takes the most energy, though it may seem to require the least. As the patient's hope for a peaceful death takes priority, he may become passive and quiet, retreating into his interior world. Try not to take offense. Having accepted death, he is turning away from life and is preparing for the final transition. You can help by respecting that his strongest advocate and ally in this busy preparation is his own dynamic inner reality of hope.

The power of hope at this stage is in looking forward or anticipating and expecting the best outcome, not for life, but for a death that is peaceful on all levels. But before the dying person can fully access the positive energy available in this kind of hoping, the roadblocks have to be removed.

It is at this time, when death becomes more real, that a process called "life review" may occur. This is when the person who is dying takes stock of his life and its many roles—such as who he has been to himself and others; what he has done or accomplished; what is left undone. Has he done enough? Been enough? Is he still thinking, "If only...," as he looks back over his time on Earth. How will he be remembered, for good or ill? Or, more important, will he be remembered at all?

The understanding, acceptance, and resolution of one's life review has a direct bearing on the type and intensity of pain one might experience before arriving at a peaceful death. Since this review plays a pivotal role in both pre-death behavior and post-death fears which impact the life-into-death experience, I will discuss it here in relation to the levels of pain that emerge from this process.

Four Levels of Pain

Basically, a peaceful death, or "a good death," requires the absence of pain on four levels. This chapter should guide you in assisting the dying person on this final leg of the journey. You'll learn how to help the dying achieve relief on these levels:

- first, *physical pain,*
- second, *emotional pain,*
- third, and perhaps the most excruciating, the *pain of mental anguish,*
- and last, the *pain of spiritual alienation.*

What's required in letting go of life peacefully—what allows one to hope for the best in whatever lies beyond death—varies in its specifics for each individual. It is essential, in assisting the patient in managing his pain, that we help him find the root of the pain; from what level or levels does it originate? Once this is known, the most effective method to bringing relief can be employed.

As in the four stages of hope, the four levels of pain often overlap and spiral back and forth continuously before resolving themselves.

The important question at this stage of hope, hope for a peaceful death (and at each level of pain), is: What would make death a peaceful prospect *for this individual?*

Relief from the primary or most-felt pain of the moment is the prerequisite for achieving peace on every subsequent level, and so, first and foremost, caregivers need to help eliminate, or at least modify, the presence of pain on the physical level. Physical pain distorts the experience of both life and death. It becomes a barrier to not only the peacefulness hoped for at life's end, but also the unexpected growth that can happen. Of course, excessively strong doses of painkillers can distort a patient's perception as well—and sap the energy they need to make the final transition. So, finding the right balance of pain medication—and monitoring it so as to keep it in balance—is of primary importance at this stage. Keeping the patient as comfortable as possible, while allowing for some alertness, lays the foundation for him to do the rest of his work.

The second level of pain is emotional pain. This often develops due to:

• strained relationships, perhaps due to unresolved issues,
• sadness from having to say good-bye to loved ones,
• regrets for what has been missed or for what might have been,
• social roles which will be left unfulfilled, such as not being there to help guide and protect others,
• fear of the process, and
• fear of the unknown.

Any and all of these can block peace from entering the patient's life at this time.

In my experience, the third source of pain—mental anguish—can be the most excruciating of all. Mental anguish often has its roots in emotional pain but has a more heartbreaking quality often stemming from shattered relationships—separation and alienation from loved ones—and the realization that completion or closure will not be forthcoming. Knowledge that the way one has lived his life has hurt or damaged others may also cause mental anguish. A type of fear of the hereafter often appears here: the fear of meeting those who abused or rejected the dying person in life or the fear of meeting those who were illtreated by the person dying. Comments such as, "Will my father turn his back on me, as he did in life?" and, "I'm afraid to see my mother again. I caused her so much pain in my life," are common.

The fourth level of pain is that of spiritual alienation. Attaining peace on a spiritual level is very important as life comes to an end. It can go far in overcoming all the other levels of pain. And vice versa: I've seen forgiveness and reconciliation drive away the pain of spiritual alienation in an instant. By accomplishing the mending of fences, as they attend to their needs on the emotional and mental anguish levels, the dying are taking care of the last level, making spiritual peace.

Strategies for Helping

Assist the patient manage his pain of the moment by helping him find the root of the pain: From what level does it originate? Once this is known, the most effective approach to bringing relief can be employed.

Here are some things you can do to help the dying deal with their pain:

- Show that you care in any number of ways, including by asking, "How may I help you?"
- Alleviate the fear of the unknown by explaining or having a physician or other caregiver explain what is likely to happen from here on.
- Let them know that they still have a say in what will happen in terms of care and treatment.
- Express that you are trying to appreciate what they are going through.
- Help them mend fences if necessary. Make calls to estranged relatives or friends; act as an intermediary.
- Reinsure them that their loved ones will be okay without them. Use specifics.
- Let them know that they will be remembered and missed.
- Emphasize the positive experiences and accomplishments in the person's life. De-emphasize the "what ifs" and the "if onlys."
- Encourage others to visit or call, especially those close to the person. Visits or cards from children are especially helpful.
- Assure them that they are not going to be abandoned, that someone will be available 24/7.
- Help with the writing of letters to say unsaid things to loved ones.
- Share beliefs.
- Bring in a pastoral care professional, such as their own minister.

Pain is such a uniquely individual and mysterious human experience that it is important to listen and hear, not only from where the pain of the moment stems but what it means to each person. The stories of Carmen and Marguerite presented below show how the levels relate to one another and how meeting the need based on the pain of the moment enables the other levels to be addressed.

Carmen

Carmen was one of my special patients in this category. She was in her mid-thirties, had five children, and her Stage 4 breast cancer had been diagnosed eighteen months earlier when her daughter, Carmencita (Little Carmen) was born. Carmencita's name fit her; in fact, she was the image of her mother before the ravages of the disease and treatment changed her.

Carmen and her family lived in Spanish Harlem, a very bad area...As her hospice nurse, Jeanette, our escort, and I entered her building, we stepped over garbage, needles, and bodies of people sleeping off a crack high.

When you entered Carmen's apartment, it was another world; although sparsely furnished, it was immaculate. You could eat off the floor it was so clean. How this skinny woman kept it so clean amazed me. No sooner were we inside, when "Cita" came running to us, squealing with delight. She had lovely, dark curls that bounced as she ran, a beautiful face, and the biggest, most extraordinary, sparkling dark eyes. It was in her eyes that I really saw the resemblance to her mother, but the sparkle in Big Carmen's eyes had been diminished by pain and disease.

Carmen's pain was constant: severe head pain due to the metastasis (spread) of the primary cancer to her brain. She had been treated with a Fentanyl transdermal patch at high dosages, high doses of steroids to decrease the swelling of her brain, and two short courses of radiation therapy to shrink her brain tumors. One of her most severe and distressing symptoms, in addition to pain, was projectile vomiting caused by the brain swelling. This further weakened her. Getting enough calories into her was becoming a real problem.

Jeanette was at her wit's end. When I first came in to help Carmen, she had been healthier. Now, due to the progression of the disease, Carmen was but a shadow of her former self. I greeted her with a hug. Jeanette had been using a complementary healing technique with

Nine Tips

Over the years I found that the following nine strategies are helpful to those dying, because they help us be there for them when it counts. Yet, the major value in utilizing these tips is found in their benefit to friends and family of the dying. Doing these things enables them to live on with fewer regrets, knowing they assisted the dying person and did not abandon him.

1. Visit. Don't feel awkward about what to say or do. Being there is more important than saying or doing the "right" thing.

2. Ask if they need or want anything. "How may I help you?" goes a long way in showing you care. Do your best to meet their requests.

3. Call if you can't visit. Even a telephone call maintains contact. It is important for all of us to hear a voice we recognize. Encourage others to call.

4. Send mail. Cards, letters, and pictures let them know you are thinking of them and gives them something tangible to see and read. Again, encourage others to send cards. Cards and letters from children are especially helpful.

5. Allow for silence. Let them know that there is no pressure to talk. Silence allows volumes to be said and heard.

6. Leave an object—something that has meaning to the patient—when you have to go away for a while. This may be a religious item, a colorful plant, a wedding album, or even a stuffed animal. This helps, because symbolically you are still there with them.

7. Send gifts. Select ones that signify the relationship you have had with them over the years.

8. Reassure them that they are not forgotten. Let them know that you and others are thinking about them.

9. Keep your promises. If you say you are going to do something, such as return at a certain time or meet with a doctor, make this a priority for you, as it will be for them.

Carmen called "Therapeutic Touch," which had been helping with the pain until now.

Jeanette had been with Carmen and had experienced her changing, fluctuating hopes throughout the journey since her first surgery. Carmen asked for my help, due primarily to my question, "What are you hoping for?" "I hope for peace," Carmen told me. "Help me find peace for me and my kids and soon."

Hearing the hope for a peaceful death come up so strongly, Jeanette and I knew we had to move quickly in order to help Carmen. We sat on the cot that was Carmen's bed. I was on the left side, holding her hand and gently rubbing her back. Jeanette was on her right, with Carmen's head on her shoulder, her right hand clasping Carmen's hand. Then suddenly Carmen tightened up, squeezing our hands. She took a deep breath and let out a scream that I have never heard before and hope I never hear again. It came from deep within her soul and filled the room with pain and anguish. She spoke in a scream, "How can I leave them? I was an orphan myself!" Upon hearing this, we were all crying. Carmen's male companion came in to help and Cita was crying, too. She ran to pat her mommy and hug her.

We just kept sitting there in shock, rocking and crying, patting and rubbing. Then, after what seemed like an eternity, I heard Jeanette say, "I didn't know you were an orphan. How can we help you with the kids?"

Through tears and deep breathing, Carmen told us that two children had the same father, but the other three each had different fathers. She made it quite clear who should go with whom after her death. As we spoke, relief and clarity began to flood through us and through Carmen. Her pain, though, manifested on the physical plane, stemmed from her love-need bonds, her emotions and, primarily, her mental anguish: "How can I leave them?"

Once we knew the root cause of Carmen's pain, relief fell into place. From her cry for help we knew she needed to put into writing—legally—who she, as the custodial parent, wanted to raise each of her children. The biggest problem we faced, however, was getting a lawyer to come to her apartment. After six or so lawyers said no, the hospice program made arrangements for a lawyer to meet Carmen, her mother, Jeanette, myself, and our social worker at the hospital when Carmen next went for radiation therapy.

Very quickly, Carmen's hope for a peaceful death was being put into place and her physical pain decreased remarkably.

But we weren't finished. On our next visit, Carmen turned to Jeanette, the social worker who had come with us, and me. "You know real peace only comes when you and God are on good terms," she told us. "So, before I can leave, I need to have Little Carmen baptized. Then my work is done."

We had a wonderful pastoral care gentleman on the team who came to see Carmen. They clicked. Carmen was able to confess and release her past. The hospice team got excited. This man had performed many funerals and several marriages, but this would be his first baptism in a hospice program.

It was by far the most joyous, lively, love-filled baptism I have ever witnessed. In the Puerto Rican tradition, baptism is held in high regard, as the children are welcomed into both the natural and spiritual family in a special way. We were all given lovely favors with lace and "Carmencita" written on beautiful blue ribbon in gold. I still have that memento from one of my most special teachers.

Carmen's pain originated from several levels and she taught me that each person is like an onion. We need to help them trust us enough to encourage them to peel away all the layers of their pain so their hope for a peaceful death may become a reality.

Carmen wrote each of her children a letter to be opened when the child turned thirteen, and her pain decreased as she finished each letter. She died with minimal pain, surrounded by her children, mother, friends, and Jeanette—her faithful nurse—to the end. Carmen also had letters for both Jeanette and me. I still treasure mine.

Marguerite

I met Marguerite when she came to be evaluated for external and internal radiation for cancer of the uterus. She finished her external course of treatment with no complications and was encouraged by this news. She was thrilled when I told her I had set up a cesium hotline to work as a support network for women undergoing internal radiation with cesium implants in the uterine cavity (a form of radiation therapy). At that time, this procedure was given over several days and the patient was isolated in a special room with minimal visitors and interaction, due to the effects of the radiation. This was scary for those receiving the treatment, and to help patients cope, I encouraged them to stay connected with each other via calls, the lending of books, and the like. After her discharge from treatment, I had left that department and Marguerite took over coordinating the program.

Nearly two-and-a-half years later, Marguerite was again my patient in the Visiting Nurse Service Hospice Program. The cancer had spread and there was no more curative treatment for her. She had a huge belly, which needed to be drained frequently, and her legs were swollen to three times their original size. She often had difficulty breathing and had pain from the fluid pressure. I was called in to help with her pain management. We made arrangements for her son to come home from the service to "see her one more time before…" They had a lovely visit and we were able to keep her comfortable. After his visit the hospice team thought things might change for Marguerite since she had been able to say her good-byes and tell her son—the only family she had left—about her affairs.

Even with all the pain, fluid retention, difficulty breathing, etc. she never complained.

Her legs began to leak clear fluid, and one day, while I was changing her many dressings, I told her, "I'm so glad your son was able to get to see you. Is there anything else you are hoping for now?"

"I hope to have the strength to endure this to the end," she told me. "How can I help you?" I asked her. With that question, she grabbed my hands and whispered in my ear, "I'm not welcome in Heaven."

"You're not welcome in Heaven, Marguerite?" I asked.

Looking me straight in the eye and still whispering, she said "I'm not forgivable. That is why I got this cancer and I have to suffer." She sighed and held my hands even tighter and looked even more intently, deeply into my eyes. "Cathy, I had an abortion when I was a teenager. I just knew I couldn't raise a child. I was a child myself. I had no other choice."

Tears welled up in our eyes and we just clung to each other. She began sobbing and I held her until she stopped. When she looked up, she was a vision of peace and relief. I said to her, "Is it enough that you have shared this with me or do you need to speak to a priest, rabbi, pastor, or anyone else?" She answered, "No, Cathy, it's enough that I was finally able to say it out loud to someone else. Thank you for listening and not saying anything when I told you my secret." She had carried it for fifty years.

Being able to finally share her secret was essential to allow Marguerite to come to a peaceful death. I don't think I realized the true meaning of being an accepting, open, listening empty slate until that magical day when I saw freedom flowing in and filling Marguerite with profound joy. Her physical pain decreased greatly after that. She did die peacefully not long after. Her newly-discharged son and I were with her. I know she waited for me to return from vacation, as she had told me she would, for our final good-bye.

What Marguerite shared with me is what I call "sacred material," and it must be treated as such. Therefore, when we chart such an interaction or report it at a team meeting, we just need to say something like, "…shared something very important with me today and saying it brought great relief and peace." The details need not be told; the client's privacy and secrets remaining confidential.

Marguerite was a special teacher for patience and silence to me. I hope her story helps you listen and hear in a special way those in your care, be it family members, friends, or patients.

At this point, death often comes quickly to the patient who is now open to it. They are often filled with the serenity of acceptance. Many of the dying have told me that, from this serenity, "helpmates," emerge for them, bringing uplifting thoughts or images that promise to lend a hand in crossing over, bringing them great joy.

Coma as a Choice

I would now like to present and discuss a phenomenon that has become clearer and clearer to me over the years as I have accompanied the dying on their final journey. It is the reality of coma as a choice, rather than merely a response to physiological changes in the dying person. Early on in my career as a Nursing Sister of the Sick Poor, as I sat with and observed the dying in their own homes, I became fascinated with the differences in how the dying process took place. I found the going into a coma or not going into a coma was something that peaked my curiosity. Why did some patients go into this state at the end of their lives, while others did not? I made some cursory observations and notes about these patients and their families at that time, but drew no conclusions.

When, during the mid-1970s, I was the director of nursing at Calvary Hospital, a specialized hospital caring for the advanced cancer patient, I found that my interest in the phenomenon of coma was once again aroused. I began to do my own very informal study as I attended rounds on the patient wards. Two hundred patients were cared for at any given time at Calvary Hospital, many with the same cancer diagnosis, so I had many patients to choose from, as well as on-site laboratory facilities.

I was able to compare patients with the same diagnoses, similar ages and similar blood work over a six-month period. What I learned from that very rudimentary observation was that entering a comatose state did not appear to be determined by changes in the patients' blood, organ function, or disease process, but rather in the realization of the patient that their loved ones needed more time to prepare for the reality of death.

As I looked at the results of my inquiry, suddenly it all came together. With a smile, I silently thanked all the patients whom I had the privilege to care for at this special time in their lives and for the lessons they taught me. It became clear to me that coma is often used by the dying when all the symbolic verbal and nonverbal language has failed, and their family just can't let them go. Coma is a dress rehearsal for their death.

Coma is utilized by the dying to gently prepare families and give them the time they need to say "good-bye;" "I love you;" "I'm sorry;" "forgive me;" "I forgive you;" "thank you;" or whatever else is needed.

Initially, when the person first goes into a coma, we hear their loved ones say, "When will they wake up?" or "They look like they are sleeping." Time passes—the length differs for each patient, family situation, and need—then we hear family members say, "Gee, they look so peaceful now, they don't seem to be suffering anymore."

As more time passes, we begin to hear the family speaking about the person in the past tense as if they were no longer there with them. Shortly thereafter the person dies. How wise are our teachers, the dying, and how gently they lead us and help us to envision their death and thus be prepared for it. Coma looks just like the sleep of death. It is the absence of physical suffering and the appearance of being asleep that helps us be able to let them go into death.

I have observed the phenomenon of patients going into comas many times over the past forty years in a variety of situations. I have seen it frequently in people who have been ill with a chronic or terminal illness, in people following normally lifesaving surgery that went awry, as well as in people following a sudden traumatic accident. Let me now share with you several powerful, poignant, and preparatory messages spoken silently by those who have made the choice of coma, as their final gift to those they love.

My first example is that of a little girl hit by a car who, due to the extent of her injuries, should have been dead on arrival to the emergency room. Instead, to the amazement of the entire medical team, she survived and lapsed into a coma, thus, giving her family, especially her parents, time to adjust to the shock. This gave them time to say their good-byes and helped prepare them for her death. Over the time she was in the coma, her parents began to slowly accept the fact that she would not have wanted to live with the disabilities she suffered from the accident, and thereby they could accept her death a little easier.

Scott

After a diving accident that should have killed Scott, an active teenager, or at the least left him a quadriplegic, the coma he entered enabled all involved to say to him what they needed. In the end, his mother freed him by saying, "Go home, Scott. You always told Dad and me after Jim's accident, 'If I'm ever paralyzed like that, please let me go.' It's tearing me apart to see you like this; they tell me you're not suffering, so I can let you go. I know it's your choice."

Paul

One of the most powerful examples of coma as a choice came from one of the patients at Calvary Hospital. We made a point of celebrating life events and especially the birthdays of our patients. As was our way, we began to discuss how Paul, one of our favorite and longtime patients, wanted to celebrate his birthday, including his choice of an everything-chocolate cake. Suddenly, or so it seemed to us, Paul went into a coma for no apparent reason. His coma lasted for six weeks. It didn't seem possible for him to know day from night and the passage of time, yet he lived until his birthday. Not for a party and his everything-chocolate cake, but so that his wife would receive his social security and pension benefits. In addition, it gave her just enough time to be eligible for senior-citizen housing so she could sell their family home.

Paul took care of her and protected her in death as he had in life. They had been married for almost fifty years and as they both had said many times, they lived for each other. However, as the weeks went by, Helen, seeing him so peaceful and no longer suffering the severe pain that had racked his body for so long, was finally able to say, "Good-bye, thank you for being my husband; I love you and now go home to your maker; I'll always love you but now I know I can go on by myself." With these loving words, Paul's wife was able to give him her permission to let go and die. At one point, I remember her saying, "Paul, it's okay for you to celebrate your birthday in Heaven, with your God."

This example demonstrated to me and now, I hope, to you, the uncanny wisdom of the dying and their knowing exactly how much time their loved ones need in order to let them go.

Diana

My final example concerns Diana, the mother of a young teenager who attended a high school bereavement group that I facilitated. Diana had been diagnosed with a brain aneurysm and was being closely monitored by her doctor and surgeons. She and the family had been told she was an excellent candidate for this surgery, as she was in her forties and very healthy. Her brother had died suddenly two years before, followed by her mother, whom she was very close to, and an aunt who had died within the last six months. Her husband was not well and she was looking forward to the surgery, as she had been suffering with headaches from the aneurysm and had not been able to help him or be there for her daughter over the last several months.

The surgery was performed on schedule but she never woke up after the operation. The family was devastated and in shock, as were her doctors, who said, this should not have happened. Diana remained in a comatose state for several weeks. While still reeling from the terrible shock, her family came to see her and say their good-byes, as they had been unable to do with her brother, the teen's favorite uncle. Miraculously, there were no other organ problems or deterioration after her surgery, which was extremely unusual following this operation. Diana's husband and daughter were able to say what they needed to say during this time and were encouraged to do so by the nursing staff.

This was essential for her daughter, as they were having some of the usual mother-teenage daughter problems and she needed to tell her mother how much she loved and appreciated her, to express her remorse for her past behavior.

Diana remained in coma just long enough for tissue typing, which enabled her to donate a kidney to her sister who was on dialysis. Just when her family was being asked to consider her quality of life and they began to talk over her and about her as if she were not there, she gently and quietly died, with her daughter and her favorite sister singing to her. In dying when, how, and the way she did, she spared her family the agony of having to make difficult decisions as had been her pattern in life. For her daughter, having the time to finish her business, say her good-byes, and be with her mother, singing to her as she died, signified her mother's final gift of love to her. Having the time to do this made the daughter's grief and bereavement process much less difficult than if her mother had died suddenly on the operating table.

Coma as a Gift

The dying, who have chosen this powerful nonverbal language, have taught me how important it is for those of us who are health care providers to teach, support, and encourage families to not waste the gift of a coma. I explain that hearing is one of the first senses we experience when we enter this world and one of the last to go when we leave it. I encourage them to take advantage of this precious time, using it to finish their business with the person who is dying.

Time after time I have had loved ones say to me, "But Cathy, I don't know what to say to them." In order to help with this, I devised a special strategy. I believe it has helped many people.

First, I tell the family member to try to put himself into the mind and thoughts of the person dying and to look at himself through the dying person's eyes. Next, I ask him to try to think of what it is that the dying person *needs* to hear him say that will allow the dying person to let go. Then, and this is equally, if not more important for the family member than the first question, I suggest he ask himself what does *he* need to say to this person in order to finish his business so he can let this loved one go to his or her death in peace.

Being able to say these important things to the dying while they are alive often eases people's bereavement process. They are saved from having to symbolically say that which they need to by letter-writing or other rituals after the death. Saying what we need to say, post-death, can also prolong the grief process.

It is my hope that you understand and resonate with these examples and that you will share this knowledge of coma as a parting gift of love with all you know who are experiencing a death in their family.

Terminal Agitation

The final separation behavior I would like to present and discuss is called "terminal agitation." It occurs just prior to the actual death and is characterized by severe agitation and high anxiety with or without physical discomfort. This occurrence is very upsetting for the family and is extremely challenging for caregivers, professional and non-professional, alike. From my experience and observation, in terminal agitation, the struggle is within the dying themselves. It is the final struggle between the body and the spirit. It is the body saying, "I can't do it anymore," and the spirit saying, "I must stay; I can't leave now." It is a graphic description of the final essential ambivalence between holding on and letting go.

Although I have seen it in elderly patients who were leaving sick or dependent spouses they were caring for, I have seen it most often and more dramatically in younger patients—usually in their thirties and forties—who were leaving a spouse or young children. Often, these patients were long-term cancer survivors, having endured many surgeries, chemotherapy, and radiation. Youth had been on their side, but at the end, the spirit was still willing but the body was weak, weakened by all the treatments and pain they had endured.

To help this come alive for you, I would like to share two examples.

The first story tells of a young father with neurofibroma of many years duration. Since adolescence, he had suffered pain of varying intensities, multiple surgeries, radiation, and chemotherapy. He came into hospice with insufficient medications for his severe pain, but his pain was soon controlled by the hospice team. The patient became peaceful, pain-free, and alert. Although his wife had not been sure she could honor his wishes that he stay at home with his family until the end, with the help and support of the hospice team and her family, she decided she could keep him at home.

During this time she gave him permission to die by saying, "You know how much the girls and I love you, but I just can't see you staying and suffering anymore." Their three girls, who ranged from two to ten years old, with the help of a bereavement counselor, made cards for their daddy and told him they loved him.

Eventually he became increasingly restless and, as death became more and more real to him, terminal agitation began. At one point he said, "It's just so hard to say good-bye to the kids; I wanted to be here to see them grow up." Exhausted after several days of this restlessness, he suddenly became calmer and, surrounded by his girls, wife, mother, and sister he quietly slipped away. At last, his struggle had ended.

The second example is of a young wife in her mid-forties, who had been battling breast cancer for several years and had tried everything she could, including experimental therapies. It was the second marriage for her and her husband, and they had both found "the love of a lifetime."

"We live for each other," her husband frequently said. "I don't think I can go on without her."

She had been on hospice for almost six months, her pain control like a roller coaster ride, when terminal agitation set in. She requested to see the pastoral counselor and told him, "I've been everything to him; I'm afraid he won't be able to make it without me and our love." And he was unrelenting in his hope, stating, "She's a fighter; she'll pull through again."

As her agitation continued, he eventually questioned her quality of life. Finally, with the help of the hospice nurse and chaplain, he finally was able to tell her, "I'll miss you and always love you, but I'll be able to go on without you somehow. By enduring all the suffering you have all these years, you have given me the courage to go on without you." Upon hearing him say these words, her agitation ceased, she breathed a deep sigh, and died peacefully, cradled in her husband's loving embrace.

Chapter 6

Wisdom of the Dying and the Choice of the Moment

How important is it to be present at the moment of death? You may think that your spouse (or mother, father, daughter, son, grandmother) is counting on you to be there. Yet more often than not, the person closest to the dying, the most beloved one, is not in the room at the final moment of passage. Why is this so? And how can you bear it, when your commitment is not to abandon them? In a moment, I'm going to explain why you need not feel you've abandoned them—or that they've abandoned you—if you are not there at the bedside at the moment of death.

The point is you have no choice in the matter. However, the dying often do.

In this chapter, I share a phenomenon, taught to me by the dying themselves: how they choose the moment they leave the earth, and who they want to be with them at that moment.

In my workshops I ask, "How many of you were with the person you loved when they died, and how did you feel being with them at that moment?" I am struck by how universal the responses are: "It was an honor." "She died holding my hand." "I crawled into bed with him and held him till he died." "Wonderful." "Scared, sad, but glad." "My aunt and I sang her into death just as she sang me to sleep as a child."

And then, I ask those who were not there at that moment, "How did that make you feel?" Again, people give such similar responses: "Terrible."

"I failed him."

"Guilty."

"She rallied, so we thought it was okay to leave her."

"He woke up and sent us to get something to eat."

"My son told me to go home, saying Jimmy needed me more than he did."

"If only I hadn't been so tired."

"If only I hadn't gone to have that cup of coffee."

The "if only" syndrome cuts to the quick of many of the survivors of this world. How well I know it. My father died suddenly when I was nineteen, and I wasn't there. My mother was ill for several years in a nursing home. All of her five children and eleven grandchildren visited her at Easter one year and, kissing us, she said, "I love you" to each of us and then she said, "Good-bye."

Now, we are not a good-bye family; we're a so-long-see-you-later kind of family. But I didn't hear the difference that day. Even having taught the symbolic language of the dying in dozens of workshops by that time, I didn't hear the finality in her message of love; I didn't interpret this as her way of preparing us for her death, as well as sparing us the pain of the actual moment.

I didn't hear it because I couldn't hear it. At that final farewell, I wasn't her nurse, a teacher on death and dying. I was just her daughter. I didn't want to hear her good-bye because that would mean she was really going to die and hearing that would be too painful. She died peacefully two days later. When I received word of her death, it didn't matter that I was the consummate professional on duty in my serene director of nursing office…and, in a totally unprofessional but completely human manner, I screamed.

I learned an important lesson at that moment, one that has helped me in my work with dying people and their families ever since. I learned that every death is a sudden death to the families of the dying. It didn't make any difference that my mother had been ill for several years and that I knew she might die at any time. I thought I was prepared, but when it actually happened I was shocked. I also learned that two people could be at the same stage of their hope systems in hoping for a peaceful death, but your vision of how that might transpire is probably not the same as your loved one's.

In some way, the dying may know what is better for them—and for us—than we do. Our vision of their peaceful passage may well include ourselves at the loved one's side. But in the final moment, we have no more control over the choice of the moment of life's end than we do over the outcome. How a person dies is as individual as how he's lived. And no matter how well you know him—or yourself— you can't predict when he'll go or how you're going to react at the last breath. On some level, every death is sudden, and no matter how you anticipate you'll react to it, you can't really know till it happens.

But the dying may know.

In my observation—and I'm not alone in noting this—the dying seem to understand and anticipate, better than we do, how we're going to feel and react to their death. I've seen it time and time again: The dying seem to choose their moment of death. And intuitively, they know the person or persons who are able to be with them at that moment, and those who can't handle it.

Statistically, most deaths occur in the middle of the night. I see this as yet another example of how the dying protect those closest to them. Operating from some depth of internal wisdom, they manage this final gift of love: to spare you the pain of the moment of the final separation.

I ask people at my workshops, "As you look back, since time has passed, do you think you could have coped with being there at that moment?" I've taught hundreds of workshops on both sides of the Atlantic, and the answer is the same: "I wanted to be there; I really did. But in all honesty, I'm not sure I could have stayed until he died."

You see, the dying are very wise. They are acutely aware that there is something very powerful in the moment of death, and they "send us out for coffee." There are several reasons the dying choose when and around whom they make their final passage. It may simply be that they are selecting those who need to be spared the physical or emotional pain of witnessing the actual moment. But the dying also recognize when we're not able to let them go, so they depart when we're not there to hold onto them. Oftentimes, they wisely choose someone else to take our place, someone not as personally attached to them.

In this way, they spare us not only the pain of bearing witness but also the burden of wondering whether they felt we had abandoned them at the end. This explains the expressions of relief that

71

I've heard so many times—remarks like, "Even though I wasn't there, I'm so glad he didn't die alone," or "I'm so happy his favorite nurse was holding his hand at the end."

The dying's choice of the moment of death can be as varied and as unique as their lives have been. Yet the manner in which they have treated others or the roles they have played in life often are borne out in both their timing and choice of companion at the very last moment. Frequently, for example, if a person has been the "protector" in life, then he waits for the arrival of another protector—someone he knows and trusts—to be there for his loved ones at the moment of his death and to be there to comfort them afterwards.

I have seen dying people hold out against all odds, choosing to wait for their favorite nurse, home-health aide, or chaplain, to be with them at the moment of their death. In this instance, their wisdom is twofold: first because the dying person had a special relationship with them, and second because this person would be there to help their families deal with their death. I have seen countless examples of parents waiting for the oldest or the most responsible child to arrive, to support their spouse before they die. Armed with an uncanny wisdom, many stay alive until the strongest person arrives before letting go.

They choose not to die on Thanksgiving, Christmas, or anyone's birthday. They hang on by a thread until the day after a special event. I have heard the bereaved say things like, "My dad chose my birthday to die because I was special and he knew I would never forget him." "I'm so glad he didn't die on our anniversary." "He didn't want to ruin my wedding, so he hung on until I was on my honeymoon."

The dying wait, far beyond medical expectations—"We don't know what is keeping her alive; she should have been dead by now." They wait for that special child, for the birth of a first grandchild, for people to return from the armed services, or traveling from far away. They hold on for a child to ask for forgiveness, to reconcile themselves with others or with God, or simply to say that special "Goodbye," or "I love you," whatever will bring peace to their survivors or to themselves. These examples show just how inextricably linked the last two stages of hope are.

The hope for prolongation of life will last as long as it takes for the dying and their loved ones both to achieve the peace they each desire. When this happens, it makes the grieving process of their survivors far easier, because they and the dying have both completed their final business.

The dying may also be waiting for their families to give them permission to leave. Therefore, it is most important that they hear loved ones say:

"I'll be all right; you don't have to worry about me."

"It's okay for you to go. I'll miss you but I know we'll meet again."

"I don't want to let you go but I know it's your time to leave me."

"I'm okay, I can balance the checkbook now!"

Sometimes, the silence of a coma speaks for the dying, as we discussed in the previous chapter. We learned how the dying who are in coma seem to know exactly how much time is needed for their loved ones to be able to release them. The coma has passively, yet powerfully, prepared them, and peaceful death comes at last. I have seen this frequently and dramatically with our hospice families. The patient awakens from a semicoma or coma, sends the spouse on an errand, for a meal or coffee or to bed, saying he is comfortable. As soon as the loved one has bustled away in relief—sometimes within minutes—the patient dies.

As a witness to events that cannot be medically explained, at the time of thousands of deaths, I've recognized that children are the clearest teachers of this innate knowledge. They are not as cluttered as adults, and the messages come right through them. I have seen children awaken from a semicomatose or comatose state, ask for their favorite food (usually ice cream), then signal their families to return home. Mission accomplished, they fall back asleep and into death in a very short time, sometimes as soon as the parent or family member is walking out the hospital door.

Often, as in the story that follows, the dying separate from those closest to them, in order to spare them the actual moment of their death. My working definition of "closest" is the presence of a bond based on love and need. Called the "love-need bond," it characterizes a relationship in which your need for the other person is equal to your love for them. The bond is very intense in the mother-child and the sibling relationships, as I'll explore in greater detail in the following chapter on the hope system of the family. But for now, I'd like to tell you about a tiny and very special teacher of mine named Danny.

Danny

Danny was only three years old and he had a fibrosarcoma of the lung that had spread to his brain. As this was an unusual cancer in one so young, Danny had undergone numerous treatments at the world-renowned Memorial-Sloan Kettering Cancer Center in New York City, even though his family lived two hours away on Long Island. I had two roles with this family: I was the night nurse, and I was also a counselor to help them face the crisis of terminal illness in one so young.

When I met Danny he had already endured surgery, radiation, and chemotherapy. Our meeting took place when he came home after his fifth admission to the hospital. Due to the progression of the disease into his brain, Danny was now blind and deaf; thus our major form of communication with him was by touch.

Touch and body language, as we learned in Chapter 4, often become the primary language of the dying as the unrelenting progression of the disease cuts off various avenues of the senses and other normal ways of expression. Therefore, we used many finger foods that the child could pick up and feed to himself. Although many years have passed, I think of Danny every time I see Cheerios—how much he enjoyed eating that cereal! In the midst of the overwhelming devastation of his illness, we all felt such joy to see him behave as a typical toddler, covered with Cheerios from head to toe.

Another lasting impression, again tactile in nature, is the image of Danny holding onto his "corner," the smooth satin corner of a blanket that his mother had lovingly replaced over and over again in his brief life. The way he reached out for his blanket—and clung to the corner with his little hand, or rubbed his cheek with it—expressed to us in nonverbal language that he had pain and how severe it was. It signaled to us as caregivers that, in addition to medication, he needed to be rocked for comfort or walked in his stroller, as this motion soothed him.

Upon his return from the hospital after each of his prior admissions, there had always been a very special and joyful homecoming welcome and celebration between Danny and Amanda, his sister, who was six years older. However, when he came home this time, he pushed Amanda away. Needless to say this was very hard for her and she required a great deal of time and help in understanding that he was not rejecting her and her love. Rather, he was pushing her away from his illness and back into life.

In my dual role as night nurse and counselor with this family, I was constantly with them. Thus, I began to notice the pattern and its deeper meaning emerge. Normally, we see children turn away when you go to wipe their mouth or kiss them when they don't want you to. But now Danny was pushing us away, not just with one hand, but with both his hands, every time. He was not just being fussy and he was not just being a toddler; it was clearly a dismissal. I recognized this subtle shift in his actions as a symbolic separation behavior, and I sensed it was time to help prepare his mother for his death.

One morning at the end of my shift, when I was bringing Danny's laundry down to be washed, an opportunity presented itself. In the most sensitive and gentle way that I could, I suggested that Danny might be trying to prepare Amanda, and the rest of us, in the only way he knew how. I remember the sparks that flew from her eyes and the anger in her voice, directing her words, like daggers, right at me: "Prepare Amanda, prepare us for what?" she shouted, and stormed off. Softly, I retreated into the laundry room. But the seed had been planted.

It was crucial that Danny's message be delivered, so that his mother would be able to let him go. However, because she was the one closest to him, this reality would be most difficult for her to hear and accept. As the life-bearer, she had brought him into this world and was his primary caretaker now. Parents must always protect the child, and when death prevents them from accomplishing this task, they feel that they are not being true to their primary role and responsibility. Thus, they frequently respond with anger toward the messenger as well as toward the bad tidings. Therefore, because the message is so important and the dying need message-takers, it is essential that caregivers not take this anger personally (For more on this, see Chapter 8).

More poignant lessons were to come from this tiniest of teachers. Shortly after pushing Amanda away, Danny pushed away his day nurse. Next, he pushed away his grandmother, then me, the night nurse and counselor. Slowly, over a three-week period, he became progressively weaker and increasingly ill. He then had a seizure and would have to return to the hospital. I had worked in Danny's home the night before, and in the morning, after I had gotten him ready to leave, his mom came in and took my hand. Looking deeply into my eyes, she said, "I am beginning to understand what you meant that day about Danny's preparing us." The daggers were gone, and I felt the sadness and sorrow in her words and in her heart.

Accompanied by his faithful three—grandfather, mother, and father—the child was again admitted to Sloan Kettering. Once stabilized in the hospital, Danny took up where he left off, in using the separation/preparation behaviors, by physically pushing his grandfather away, which signaled his final good-bye to his "Pop-Pop." Later on, his grandfather shared his interpretation of this behavior with me: "For the first time ever, when I went to kiss him he wouldn't take my hand. He pushed it away, in a gesture that said I'm finished with you, then opened his hand and waved me away from him. I knew in my heart it was his final good-bye to me."

After sending his Pop-Pop away, Danny had been going in and out of consciousness when suddenly he awakened, drank some water for his mother, then very powerfully and clearly pushed her away. His mother decided at that moment to go and get a cup of coffee. No sooner had she left than Danny turned to his father. Grasping his blanket's corner close to his face, he reached out for his father's hand. Danny held it tightly for a long moment, then released his grip and gently pushed it away, and slipped peacefully into his death.

His mother returned and became very upset that she had not spent her child's last moments with him. Her normal feelings of sorrow and grief were intensified because, as his mother, she had been so intimately involved with his first moments. She felt that she had somehow failed him by not being with him as he breathed his last.

This moving story graphically illustrates the reality and the depth of the innate wisdom of the dying, and how they choose the moment of their death. How else could such a young child know to push away those closest to him and be able to understand their ability to cope with his death?

There is no possible way that a three-year-old could have *learned* to do this. Since such a small child exhibits such knowledge, we can confidently propose that the same profound interior wisdom operates in adults as well, when they are face-to-face with death.

Danny knew that the only person strong enough to be there for him, and yet be able to let him go, was his father. His choice of the moment of his death was to be with the person who had always been there for him with quiet strength from the moment he came into life. As he most clearly pushed his mother away, he simultaneously accomplished two important tasks that helped him die a peaceful death. First, he was doing all he could to ensure that the person holding fastest to him would be out of the room at the moment of his release. Second, because of his closeness to and love for his mother, he chose—as a final gift of love to her—to spare her the final moment, which he *knew* would be too painful for her to experience.

Studies show that the death of a child is the most difficult loss of all to cope with. It seems against nature for a child to precede the parent into death. I saw Danny's mom for bereavement counseling after her son died, and as is so often the case, the passage of time made a crucial difference. The actual moment of death can be uplifting and profound, but it is also frightening and final. Eventually, loved ones can admit, as she did, that although they wanted to be on hand at that moment, it would have been overwhelming for them. Freed by this admission, they usually realize the depth of the dying person's intuition and love for them. At last they understand what the dying so clearly know, that the anguish of parting may be more difficult for us to endure than for them.

And our anguish can make it more difficult for them. Physician and author Bernie Siegel, M.D., theorizes that most people die in the middle of the night because that's when the caregivers have left and they can die without guilt. There is no question that the dying process requires a lot of energy, and when we don't accept their hope for a peaceful death, we deny them that energy.

We may rail against the dying in the night, as we need to, after the death. And, day-by-day, there is no need to hide our grief as they slip away. Their acceptance of death may outpace ours, but we do our loved ones and ourselves a lot of good when we honor and respect their acceptance, regardless of how we feel. People don't change each other. We can only change ourselves. And in the end, just like in the beginning of this process of life and death, what makes life worthwhile is exactly this, the ability to make our own choices until the last breath.

A Conscious Choice?

Many have asked whether the choice of the moment is made consciously or unconsciously. Science is actively working on this question, but as yet we do not have a definitive answer. So far, all we can point to are the well-documented separation behaviors described in Chapter 4 which, in The Hope System, signal the transition from hope for prolongation of life to hope for a peaceful death. The primary internal force that initiates this chain of events in the patient is the cluster of physiological changes that the person is experiencing. The dying seem to register an inner knowing that their life is coming to an end. And, at some point, this inner knowledge prompts them to say "Good-bye," instead of, "So long, see you later." The precise nature of this inner knowing is still a mystery. But we see clues to how it functions within ourselves and in how the dying speak to us with their actions and behaviors, when we learn how to listen and really hear.

The dying themselves are our greatest teachers. They alone experience this unique process, and only they can impart this special knowledge. I have *been there* with literally thousands of people at the special time of their passing into death. I know on a deep level that the knowledge that the dying have so generously shared with me has been given to me for a specific reason: so I can help other professional caregivers and families recognize the deeper meaning in the choice of the moment of death as the person's final gift of love.

As I have shared this understanding in my workshops and with thousands of dying patients and families over the years, it has become clear to me that when we understand the wisdom of the dying and the choice of the moment of death, we are relieved of the burdens of guilt and the if-only syndrome. This understanding helps immensely in the grieving process.

While I don't presume to speak for them—the dying speak for themselves—in this instance, allow me to take this message to you on their behalf: As you read this, if it strikes a familiar chord and even brings forth tears, I entreat you to let go of any feelings you might have that you abandoned a loved one. We do not abandon the dying. The choice of the moment is not ours to make. It belongs to the dying.

And, to take the logic one step further, they do not abandon us, either. In their final act, by the choices they make, they do what they feel is best for us, whether that is to be with them at their side, or not. If they are allowed to, they choose the timing of their death as an affirmation of their life and their love for us.

And then it becomes our turn to release whatever *we* need to release. We can take that affirmation and run with it: As the living, we can choose to put regret and guilt aside and live with intensity until we die, just like the dying teach us to do. That is our decision to make, our own choice. The rest is out of our hands. So if your thoughts and feelings of guilt have weighed heavily upon you, release yourself from them as your loved one has released you—and released their life as well.

Our role as caregivers is to inform, affirm, and support the choices the dying make, and to recognize that these choices come from an inner wisdom. The exact thing they are hoping for changes, as they move through and around the four stages of hope. But hope itself—as the driving force of their inner reality—never changes. The act of hoping—looking forward, expecting the best—is synonymous with living and it continues until the moment of death. No matter how much courage seems to falter, hope prevails even over fear into our last moments.

In pushing you away, the dying are directing you back toward life, and away from death—because they know that is where you belong.

At the same time, the dying are also clearing a space for themselves to turn in their own direction, as they travel deeper on their inner journey. In fact, although they may seem absolutely passive, the dying are actually very busy. They are looking within and, perhaps, ahead. We commonly describe their condition as without hope, yet they are full of hope.

It is hope's role, and not ours, to conquer this fear of the unknown that may affect the dying, and hope intensifies accordingly at the end to help make this death a peaceful one. At the end, hope is all that the dying have left—but it is more than enough.

Chapter 7

The Hope System and Loved Ones

In the previous chapters, I described The Hope System as it applies to the patient in detail. Now I would like to turn my focus to The Hope System as it applies to the significant others who have a relationship with the dying person.

It is a crucial element in our discussion here that the dying and their family and loved ones be considered as a single unit, much as mother and child are often addressed as one. The significance of our viewing them in this integrated way has a direct relationship to their hope systems. They should be seen in this way because, in a unique and special way, they are all dying.

The expression that most aptly describes this special relationship is "closeness." As I mentioned in the previous chapter, my working definition of closeness is the presence of a love-need bond. We often hear family members and others closest to the dying express this bond: "Not only is she my mother, she is my best friend." We may hear a woman speak lovingly of her husband: "He is not only my husband, but my strength. He has always been my protector."

Often caregivers enter the patient's room and find the dying person sleeping soundly while the spouse of twenty, thirty, or even fifty years sits beside him or her in tears. In effect, the person who is dying with the greatest intensity at that moment is the spouse, not the patient who is sleeping peacefully.

It is important that we who are caregivers, either as part of our personal or professional role, understand this fact clearly if we are to be effective helpers. Understanding that, in a special way, each is dying enables us to shift our focus to all parties. Sometimes we have difficulty with this because we were taught that the dying patient is our primary focus and responsibility. While this is true, since all are dying, all need understanding, help, and support to deal with the dying process and its ultimate outcome.

Bearing this shared need for support in mind, also realize that family members tend to be somewhat more consistent with the first three hopes than the patient; that is, they maintain a more constant hope for cure, hope for treatment, and hope for prolongation of life. They do not seem to fluctuate as much as patients do. This is because they are not continually bombarded by doctors and other health professionals presenting new treatments, discussions, or other possibilities. Families seem to respond more to the bond of their relationship with the patient than to the process or changes in the treatment regimen.

At different ages and developmental periods in our lives, our love and need bonds change, as they do in times of stress and crisis. The crisis of impending death causes the intensity of these bonds to increase dramatically.

This significant love-need relationship responds to the special and unique sustenance needs of the patient throughout his illness. Hope is nourished by communion with others. Friends and family can spark hope that those who love and need him are waiting for him to return home.

On the other hand, the dying person's hopes for cure or treatment stokes his loved ones' desire to accompany him through the most rigorous of therapies even when they know he will not return to his previous physical level.

Hope for prolongation of life offers the possibility that they can have a new, enriched life together despite severe physical changes or disease progression.

It is definitely these hopes transmitted by the family, coupled with the person's own hope system, that enables the dying to undergo difficult and devastating treatments and live through them. People's ability to withstand so many debilitating surgeries and therapies demonstrate that hope and love do more than simply coexist.

Support for the Family

Since the loved one's role is so important to the life potential and development of the patient, support for the family members is essential and can take several forms. These include education, especially in the all-important interpreting and translation of a patient's hopes. Changes experienced by a dying patient cover the range of physical, emotional, psychological, and spiritual planes. At this time the patient is especially vulnerable and often deeply connected to the love-need bonds of those who are closest to him.

The always-necessary listening presence includes counseling the patient as needed, which has a direct and beneficial effect on him as well as those close to him. If the family feels informed and confident of outcomes—both negative and positive—these feelings are readily conveyed to the patient. They can sustain him throughout the death process, no matter how difficult it may be at each moment.

The caregiver's sharing of knowledge and observations with the family on a continual basis, which I call the "communication loop," teaches the family to tune in and hear the subtle nuances that indicate changes in the patient's hopes for himself *and* their hopes for him. They learn to be open to hear the movement from hope for cure or treatment, to hope for prolongation of life, and finally to hope for a peaceful death both within the patient and within themselves.

Protective Coping Denial

The closer and more bonded people are, the greater the difficulty everyone has in letting go. Intense love-need bonding makes the thought of separating all the more painful for both parties.

Those closest to the dying have the greatest difficulty in accepting or coming to terms with the death. They often experience intense denial while trying to accept the diagnosis, the dying process, and ultimately the death itself.

If we understand the love-need bond, then we can understand the need for and mechanism of the family's denial. It is just too painful for them to think or let into their consciousness that their loved one could possibly die and leave them. Those closest to the patient often maintain the initial shock, disbelief, and denial stage for a long time.

I have named this initial or lead-in denial *protective coping denial*. Denial—our universal coping mechanism—comes into play from the moment of diagnosis. While acknowledging the presence of a change in the body, such as the presence of lumps, abnormal discharge, bleeding, or other symptoms, both the patient and family are protected from the too-painful fact that this presence may signify or herald the reality of death. The closer the bonds, the more intense and prolonged the denial.

Usually, after a while, both the patient and those near and dear to him are able to let down the protective shields of their denial to allow treatment to begin. The initiation of active treatment and therapy becomes a beacon signaling that help and a possible cure are on the way.

I liken this fascinating defensive mechanism—protective coping denial—to the Lucite shield found in many of our modern banks that separates tellers from their customers. It is clear, yet quite strong, and it allows the tellers to see us as we see them. However, tellers are protected by the shield should there be any threat of danger, harm, or death. Protective coping denial acts in a similar manner, protecting patient and family from the threat of danger or death. It enables them to see the problem, seek help, and activate their own hopes for cure and treatment.

Protected by their denial, they begin to cope with the diagnosis and plunge with strength and commitment into therapeutic regimens, either as the participant or as the observer.

As time and treatments continue, the same denial reaction may become evident again as both patients and their loved ones move into what we often call the "conspiracy of silence." They move into different corrals when *he* knows and *she* knows but they don't talk about it. This behavior is seen by each as a type of protection of the other and once again stems from the love-need bond: "Because I love you, I must and will protect you from this horrible truth, this death over which I have no control."

Denial is one of the most powerful coping and protective mechanisms and we have it because we need it. Because it is so vital to our survival, it must be recognized and treated with respect. It must *never* be attacked, negated, or taken away. Removal of this important protection leaves the patient and families open and vulnerable.

Balancing Denial with Reality

On the other hand, we know how important it is for the dying and their loved ones to finish their business and say their good-byes prior to death. This communication frees the patient to die peacefully and helps the family live on more peacefully after the death has occurred. So, how can we help them to get together in one corral before it's too late?

Come with me now as Jenny and her husband, Chris, show us how they were able to accomplish this crucial task—just in time.

Jenny and Chris

Jenny was my patient for several years and was in the latter stages of rapidly advancing melanoma. She had survived many disfiguring surgeries and treatments all over the United States and Europe, empowered by her intense hope for cure and hope for treatment and supported in these hopes by her husband and their three loving children.

But the disease was taking a heavy toll on Jenny. She an her husband, Chris, both knew it, but they were protected by their denial.

I went to see Jenny and found Chris crying in the hallway. "She's not good today," he said. "I think she's losing the battle. I don't know what to do to keep her spirits up." I asked him the question he had heard many times as we shared Jenny's journey, "What are your hopes for Jenny, now?" He answered, "I hope she doesn't suffer at the end. I know I have to say good-bye to her soon."

This told me that Chris had shifted from hope for prolongation of life to hope for peaceful death for Jenny. Now I had to hear where Jenny was. Later that day she answered my query with, "I hope it's peaceful." Then, tearfully, "It's so hard to say good-bye to Chris and the kids. I have so much I need to say to them."

All of us knew that time was running out. My role as mediator/messenger could not have been clearer. Their conspiracy of silence was no longer protecting them; it was now preventing them from saying what they needed to say so that a peaceful death was possible.

To help them accomplish this task, I enlisted an approach that I have used with many families to help them align their hopes into a unified hope for a peaceful death and communicate openly.

I sought Chris out and said to him, "Chris, it's clear to me how much you love Jenny, how you have protected her and have been her cheerleader from the beginning. Things are changing and the way you are acting and speaking is making her feel left out."

There is something powerful in the expression of this thought that immediately helps the patient and/or the family to see reality clearly because we *never* want our loved ones to feel left out and we will do anything, to get them back in sync with us. Also remember we are fulfilling the first basic need of dying. They need to know they will not be abandoned.

Chris realized right away, "Oh no. I thought I was helping her and protecting her. Cathy, help me say and do what is best for her to get us back together."

"Let's start by sharing with Jenny what you shared with me this morning. I spoke to her later and she's hoping for the same things you are; it's important for you to really talk to each other now."

Relief flooded Chris' face as he thanked me and ran off to Jenny's room. My understanding of The Hope System and how it applied at this step of Jenny's journey enabled me to be the swing person and to help them accomplish this important task.

With the denial removed, Chris, Jenny, and their children were able to use the precious time they still had to complete the important tasks that would free them to be with each other, say their good-byes, and to say, "I love you."

This enabled Chris to lovingly give Jenny permission to make her transition in peace. Inspired by the openness and the example of their parents, the kids, in their own teenage ways, expressed what they needed and wanted to tell their mom. As they shared in her death, they were also helped to share feelings and support each other through their bereavement process. This was made easier because there were few, if any, regrets: "We said what we needed to and she knew we loved her to the very end."

I hope I have helped you see that the best way to deal with denial is not with a sledgehammer, but gently, using love and need, helping the patient and family to hear how their hopes have changed so that they can be there for each other and to respectively die in peace and to live on in peace.

Double-Bondedness

An intense love-need bond may be a contributing factor in the sometimes almost immediate death, for no apparent reason, of a surviving spouse after the death of his or her mate. You may have heard this situation described as someone having died from a broken heart, but it might be more accurately defined as the severing of the sustenance of the love-need bond. This double-bondedness is seen most dramatically and powerfully in the parent-child relationship, and of course, goes back to the concept of the patient and loved one both dying.

Hazel and Bobby

Perhaps the story of Hazel and Bobby will demonstrate the potential intensity of both the love-need bond and concurrent denial.

I had worked with Hazel, a young mother whose son, Bobby, was dying of leukemia, from the day of diagnosis through aggressive therapies and I was with her at the end.

Bobby did not die easily, and at the point our story begins, he had pain in his joints and throughout his body and was bleeding through several openings. The mother's loving and tender care was beautiful to behold, and as I sat with her, it was becoming clearer and clearer to me that the child was ready, and in fact, wanted to die.

I had been trying to share and interpret his nonverbal language, wishing to indicate this to her in a very gentle way. As we sat together, I used an analogy that has helped me describe denial with many patients and their loved ones.

We talked about death being like the sun, and that sometimes, in order to look at it, we have to put on sunglasses. At other times, when it appears nearer and brighter, we go indoors to escape it. At other times, when it becomes especially bright, we might not only go inside, but also pull down the shades to protect ourselves from its blinding rays. If it were then to find a way inside, we might jump into bed and pull the covers over our heads for more protection.

At that moment, tears welled up in her eyes. Slowly she picked up Bobby and cradled him in her arms saying, "All during the treatments I even threw the sunglasses away. For a while, I was all right in the shade of the treatments and the partial remission. Later the house provided enough safety until I had to pull down the shades after the bone marrow transplant failed and the leukemia was out of control.

"Eventually I thought that if I stayed inside under the covers, I could protect him forever. Even though he's bleeding and he has pain, I thought, I still have him and I can still hold him, and I will take care of him forever."

Thus we sat together, she rocking him in her arms, and I sitting next to them with one hand on her shoulder for strength and the other gently touching his head, the blonde fuzz growing back in after the chemotherapy and radiation treatments. Slowly his breathing changed as she sang to him. She called upon his guardian angel to help him on his journey and to enable her to let him go. After his breathing ceased and he gently drifted away, she kissed him and placed him on the bed. With loving hands, she covered him with a light blanket, turned to the windows and opened the blinds to let in the sun. The tears were our means of communication until she broke the silence and said, "Who will take care of him now? Am I still his mother?"

In that instant, I understood in a most powerful way the complexity of the feelings of the person closest to the dying and their need for protective coping denial throughout the dying process up to and including the very moment of death. I think that I also appreciated in a very deep way that much help is needed by the family to be able to let them go on in peace.

Feelings of Guilt

Sometimes a person's hope for a peaceful death for another is equated with wishing that this person die. One thing we as helpers must not allow is for people to think that, in the act of letting go, they have *wished* their loved one dead. How the survivors think of this time and the death itself has a direct bearing on their bereavement process and healing. If they think they wished their loved one dead, they may have the added burden of guilt, which impedes their healing.

When Roles Vary

It is important to note that the individual closest to the dying person may or may not be in a normal socially designated role, such as parent or spouse. They may not even be in a socially accepted role. This person may be anyone from the oldest, youngest, or most needy child in a family to a dear friend, illicit lover, or surrogate parent.

It is necessary for those of us acting as helpers—whether we are professional caregivers, volunteers, or family members or loved ones—to be sensitive to the closeness of relationships and to be there with compassion for all involved— and always without judgment.

Chapter 8

Especially for the Professional

I would like to turn now to the role of the professional caregiver as educator, mediator, and translator. Health-care professionals need to let their patients know that they are respected and valued as unique persons, not just as patients. With this in mind, the goal of this chapter is to show health care workers why they should support a patient's hope system, and how they can do so without compromising their professionalism.

In order to accomplish this, the caregiver must be an empty slate, allowing the dying patient to write his own story. The caregiver, as an empty slate, possesses an attitude of openness, respect, and sensitivity to patient and family. This enables the caregiver to recognize and interpret the hope systems of his patients and their families, as well as recognize his own hopes for his patients.

Caregivers have the power to be inspiriting to their patients. Sidney Jourard, a leading force in humanistic psychology, and a pioneer in the fields of self-disclosure and body-awareness, describes *inspiriting* as delivering "an invitation to continue living, to develop each individual's exquisite potential." In the case of terminal illness, the attainment of this potential culminates in a peaceful death.

Professionals can clarify and support hope in various ways, but primarily they do so by helping the patients understand and draw on the resources found in their individual hope systems. The health-care provider must determine which phase of The Hope System—hope for cure, hope for treatment, hope for prolongation of life, or hope for a peaceful death—predominates for the patient at any given moment. Once this is ascertained, it is the responsibility of the caregiver and care team to provide the patient with the supportive care needed during that phase. For example: Encouragement, information—including an explanation of the diagnosis—and treatment are essential during hope for cure and hope for treatment, as opposed to the comfort, care, palliation, and presence needed during the hope for a peaceful death phase.

It must be clear to the caregiver that the patient's hope may not be the same hope that the caregiver has for him at that time. Support of the patient's hope system is always a priority. In the terminally ill, hope becomes the patient's real world, an inner reality that takes precedence over all other realities. Hearing others deny this reality, saying it is unrealistic or unimportant, doesn't change this; it simply sends the patient's thoughts and feelings underground and frustrates the satisfaction of two basic needs: the need to not feel abandoned and the need to express one's self.

In acknowledging the validity of the patient's inner reality of hope, caregivers go a long way in supporting this process and can better accompany the patient on the final leg of his journey to a peaceful death.

Working with the Family

The fostering of sustaining relationships is also a key responsibility of the caregiver. The patient's loved ones, not the caregiver, have the most powerful influence on sustaining the patient's hopes. The caregiver should work directly with those closest to the patient initially by explaining the concept of The Hope System to them and the interrelationship between their hopes and those of the patient.

It is essential that the health-care professional attain and maintain open communication with both the family and the patient—the group interaction that I call the "circle of care." From this focal position, the caregiver can assist loved ones and help other team members clarify their hope system for the patient, thus providing additional support.

The caregiver should guide the family in personalizing their understanding of the hope system by asking, "What are you hoping for your loved one at this time?" This important query helps them grasp the reality of The Hope System from the inside out, just as it does with their loved one. This knowledge demonstrates to them how powerful they are in nurturing the individual hope system of the patient.

Mutual Trust

It is also extremely important for the health-care professional to realize how crucial her interaction with the patient is. This is especially true in the area of trust. A special bond of nonjudgmental trust between the dying patient and caregiver facilitates the open communication of the deep and essential hopes from within the patient. Because of this mutual trust, the patient knows that whatever he shares is heard and not judged. The caregiver thus becomes the empty slate, helping the dying to write his own story, dot his own *i*'s, place his own commas, and finish his life with a period, an exclamation point, or a question mark.

Watching for the Changes in Hope

Being able to perceive when the patient's hopes change is primarily the responsibility of the caregiver who can be more objective than family members since he is not as affected by love-need bonds as is the family. He takes on the roles of educator, mediator, translator, and supporter, helping both the patient and family read and understand the words written on the empty slate.

These multiple roles are essential so that the dying person's hopes for himself, as well as those of his loved ones, can each be realized. Assisting the dying person to unearth his own hope system is crucial and begins early on by explaining that both the presence and the power of hope is always active within him and that hope has been and is now making an impact on every facet of his life. His grasp of the power of hope deepens each time he is asked, "What are you hoping for?" By answering this question time after time, his awareness of the reality and power of hope within him emerges more clearly.

Doing this enables the professional caregiver to help the patient live his hope each day of his life and to bring about his final hope for a death that is peaceful on his own terms.

Being to Becoming

Hope is the activator for an individual's process of becoming, and it allows the movement from *being* to *becoming*, which is possible at every moment of human existence. Hope is like an entrance door through which we gain access to the reservoir of both our own and our patient's hope systems.

Hope not only helps to maintain our existence, but encourages us to develop our deepest potential throughout all our lives. Hope becomes stronger and all-pervasive as we proceed on our path toward death. Thus, death is seen as the final "becoming" and the last stage of human growth.

Synchrony

The professional caregiver who is in synch with the dying person and his family creates a climate in which all hopes can be realized. This is a climate that is imbued with hope and helps the caregiver to clarify his own as well as the patient's and the family's hope systems. As we have discussed, the family is a patient's main source of sustenance throughout the dying process.

Often with just a word or suggestion, the professional can help ease the dying process profoundly. For example, as I mentioned in Chapter 3, my response to Frank's final question to me—"Yes, Frank, the medication will keep you comfortable until…"—reassured him that the peaceful death he envisioned would come to pass.

Diane, a single mom who was concerned about her teenage daughter, was greatly relieved when I told her we had a social worker who has a gift with teenagers. "I'll ask her to come to see you. I know she can help you with your daughter."

Tim was a fighter all the way and I was happy to help honor his final request: "Cathy, I don't want to be snowed with medication at the end." I told him, "Tim, we have a pharmacist who will work with you and your physician to enable you to die pain-free and alert."

When we realize hope is a dynamic process among patient, family, and caregiver, we begin to understand the necessity of the caregiver to be in synchrony with each person.

The professional is in a good position to serve as an interpreter of behavior that signals a shift in the patient's hope system, a change that the family often doesn't clue into right away. The professional can be especially important in helping the family understand the movement of hope for a peaceful death into the foreground for the patient. As we've seen, enabling patient and loved ones to communicate prior to death facilitates the grief process and healing after death.

The sensitivity to and understanding of the subtle and the more overt changes in both the patient's and the loved ones' hope systems enables the professional to resonate with each in a different and unique manner. This special resonance is called the *trust relationship*, wherein both patient and family are freed to share their personal hopes aloud to the caregiver and to each other without being judged.

This is a real-life application of the caregiver's role of messenger and translator: helping each party to hear and understand the hopes of the other. Frequently, both the patient and the loved ones find it easier to share their personal hopes with an open and unbiased caregiver. Then after listening and hearing the hopes of both, and with their permission to share them, she takes the message from one to the other or brings them together to hear each other's hopes, whichever is the most helpful to each situation. This helps them hear how their hopes may differ or agree and how they may be brought into alignment with one another. This often happens with the insight and support of the caregiver guiding them.

Try as we may, some patients and families are not able to come together in mutual hope for a peaceful death for a variety of reasons. It is important to remember that people choose the way they die and the way they live, and they will have different requirements both during the dying process and after. However, if a trust relationship can be established, all are assured they will be accepted as they are regardless of the outcome.

Through all this, we need to remember that, although we create the climate by being the best nurse, social worker, doctor, home-health aide, chaplain, or volunteer we can be, it is always the patient who chooses the person or persons they trust to be there as his path twists and turns till journey's end.

Caregiver as an Authority Figure

Because of his uniform and medical expertise, the professional appears as an authority figure. What he says carries great impact. He needs to tell the truth in the form of pertinent information, of course, but he does best when he bears in mind that medical prognoses are largely based upon statistical likelihoods and that there is a deeper truth within each individual, a truth called hope.

The Hope System is an extremely dynamic process. As we've discussed, the caregiver's hope system for a patient will change as he perceives changes in the patient's clinical, psychological, and emotional state. Yet, the caregiver must simply be there for the dying. He should not tell his patient what to do or how to act or how to be. And the caregiver should never impose his own hopes on the patient just to make it easier on himself.

What Are You Hoping for?

From the moment of the diagnosis, people are asking the patient important questions:

"How are you feeling today?"

"Did you sleep last night?"

"Do you have pain?"

"How is your appetite?"

And, of course, the ever popular, "Did you have a bowel movement today?"

The answers to these questions indicate where the patient is regarding his physical condition and how his disease is progressing. And although important, they do not touch on his interior world where he lives to a greater and greater degree as his physical world deteriorates.

It is the role of the caregiver to ask, "What are you hoping for?" When we ask what the person is hoping for today, what he or she is hoping for from one treatment or another, or another similar question about his or her hopes, we cut through the person-as-patient role and connect with the deeper part of the person who is experiencing this process. Then, and equally important, when we ask the family members this same crucial question, we can learn the hopes of the loved ones supporting him.

It is important to respectfully acknowledge the patient's and their loved ones' hopes as they are expressed. When we do this, we are maintaining both the circle of care and the primary communication loop between patient, family, and caregiver.

The simple fact that both the patient and loved ones are being asked what it is they are hoping for imparts to each four important points.

- First, that the caregiver sees each individual as a unique person.
- Second, that the caregiver acknowledges and affirms that he knows this person has hope.

- Third, that the caregiver is willing and anxious to listen to each person's hopes.
- Fourth, that the caregiver accepts the patient as he is and accepts where he is at in this moment of time.

This approach frees the patient from responding in the traditional compliant-patient role and establishes a more human interaction—the trust relationship mentioned earlier—where hope can be easily shared and articulated. The usual response of the patient to this approach is to experience a sense of relief. Often it seems he has been waiting for someone to relate to him in this way: "At last someone is trying to understand me and what is important to me."

The empty slate and the trust relationship are two very effective approaches for accompanying the dying on his own path toward death in a way that frees both patient and caregiver to be true to themselves.

Ed and Tina

I was working in the radiation therapy department of a local hospital when I met Ed and Tina. It was immediately apparent how close they were. Ed was being prepped for radiation therapy to shrink a lung tumor that was pressing on his trachea, causing him pain and making it difficult to breathe. Following radiation, he would have surgery, then chemotherapy, and all would be well again. At least this is what they had "heard" their oncologist say to them.

As I sat with them, I listened to their hopes for cure and treatment. Ed said, "My brother had radiation too and he's okay. I know I'm gonna' beat this thing, just like him." Tina spoke to me while he was being tattooed so the radiation would be directed only where his tumor was and spare the surrounding tissue. "I know he'll be okay; he's such a fighter."

Unfortunately, Ed had a rough time with the radiation. His skin was sensitive so we had to interrupt his treatments to allow him time to heal. Ed said, "I'm not happy about the setback, but I know the radiation will do the trick." Tina encouraged him by saying, "I know you'll be okay Ed; you're a fighter."

Even though we had blocked his organs, Ed developed a severe tracheitis with continuous coughing. Eventually, we stopped his radiation altogether.

His response to my question, "What are you hoping for now?" was, "I'm sure the radiation worked well enough for them to do surgery." Tina's response to the same question was, "I know he'll get through this; he's a fighter."

Surgery was successfully performed and Ed started chemotherapy. Ed, at the hope for treatment stage, said "I've made it this far; I'm gonna' beat this thing." Tina supported this hope, "See, you're a fighter Ed; you'll get through this, too."

Halfway through his chemotherapy protocol, Ed came in to visit me. He was limping; his routine bone scan showed metastasis to the thoracic and lumbar areas of his spine. His response to the hope question was, "I hope the radiation can do its magic again; our daughter is getting married in June." Tina's response was, "I want him to be well enough to walk Susan down the aisle."

For this couple, hope for prolongation of life had entered the spotlight. As his disease progressed, radiation therapy offered temporary relief, and, when questioned, Ed answered, "I only hope the pain medication keeps working." Tina added, "I hope they can keep him comfortable. June is just around the corner."

Empowered by his own and Tina's constant hope for life, and with the help of more radiation and stronger medication, Ed did walk his daughter down the aisle to the joy of all concerned.

After this momentous event, Ed began a slow but steady decline. Eventually he was hospitalized for a morphine drip. At this point, hope for a peaceful death was expressed by both husband and wife. From Ed: "I hope it's over soon. I'm so tired." And from Tina: "I hope, for his sake this is all over soon. He fought the good fight."

Asking "What are you hoping for?" helped me stay connected with Ed and Tina from diagnosis until death.

Swing Person

A key attribute of a caregiver is the ability to listen and to be present to both family and patient. By identifying his own personal hope system and using it as a point of internal reference, the professional caregiver can clearly understand what he is hoping for at each interaction. This knowledge has the power to stabilize and ground him. He knows what he is feeling in relation to the patient and the patient's family, and what he is hoping for the patient at any particular time. This awareness helps to enable him to let go of his own hope system stages and thus be available to respond to the changing hopes of others as needed. He becomes the *swing person*.

It is crucial that the swing person has the ability to emotionally travel with the patient and family as hopes shift and to give the support necessary as each stage of The Hope System appears. From the secure position as the professional helper, the caregiver is able to hear beneath words and behaviors to the deeper, more consistent themes and hopes. As these messages emerge from the patient's private interior world into the light, the caregiver is able to interpret them for the dying, those closest to him, and members of the care team, as needed. This strengthens the trust relationship, allowing for increased understanding, energy exchange, and support throughout the entire process.

How May I Help You?

This approach of open inquiry has assisted me to ask another very important question, one that has helped me to enter the world of the dying person. It is simply, "How may I help you?"

This question is essential for deeper communication because, in fact, we don't truly know what individuals in our care are experiencing in their personal journeys from life into death. Asking this question, listening to the answer, not assuming or imposing, and utilizing The Hope System, has helped me work in a different, more real way with the dying. This is demonstrated in the story of young Krystal below.

We Aren't All Knowing

Being present for the dying does not mean that we know or indeed should know all the answers to the mysteries of dying and death.

My life as a helper to the dying changed dramatically when I was able to let go of the burden of the erroneous belief that I should know all of the answers, after all, "I am the professional."

What the dying *do* need, is for us to listen, hear, and respond to their pain and concerns, to really *hear* their story and, on occasion, to act as messengers, communicating their wishes and hopes to their loved ones.

Other Helpmates

There may be others, ones much more effective than you and I, in easing the profound passage from what we know as life into what we don't know. As death comes closer, the dying—whose focus now moves within—turn away from us, perhaps to another listening presence that they have recently become aware of. As this happens, they appear to be more "there" than "here with us."

Krystal

By telling the story of this young girl, I want to show one way a child reported the presence of such helpmates. Real or imagined, these hopeful visions comfort the dying through the transitional moment. The story that follows also illustrates how caregivers and loved ones can avoid becoming a distraction and can respond to this phenomenon in a way that maximizes the inner power of the dying person's hope.

Krystal was a beautiful, blue-eyed, blond-haired girl of three when I first met her in the pediatric unit of Long Island Jewish Medical Center. I remember thinking she looked like a porcelain doll because her features were so perfect. When she smiled, she lit up the room.

In my role as clinical nurse specialist in oncology and thanatology, I spent a great deal of time working with the staff of "Four South" and their little ones who were caught at a very tenuous juncture between a young life and young death.

Since caregivers should never separate the parent from the child, I became involved with the parents and other loved ones of these special patients in strollers and tiny wheel chairs. Over time, the staff and I formed a special circle of care embracing each of these tiny tots.

Such was the case with Krystal, whose blue-white sparkle was dulled by the unremitting progression of the cancer that was slowly and surely draining her life away. I had been working with mother and child for almost a year. Krystal had been in a special chemotherapy protocol for her type of leukemia. The protocol was not working and little Krystal was becoming paler and paler with each passing day.

One day, I received a call from the unit saying Krystal's mother needed me. The unspoken plea that I heard beneath the staff member's words was, "We need you, too, Cathy. We don't know what to do." At my arrival on the fourth floor, I was greeted by a staff with anguished faces and beseeching eyes. They quickly told me that Krystal had just told her mother that she had to leave soon and that her mom had to go with her.

Both Krystal's comment and her request were not only understandable, but developmentally correct for her age and her needs. For the young child, separation is viewed as death. Thus, it was perfectly natural and normal for Krystal to want and need her mom to go with her. Of course, in the magical thinking of the child, Krystal had assumed that her mother could leave with her on her final journey. Since her mother had been the most consistent parent figure for her, the two, in effect, had never been separated during Krystal's short life.

Nevertheless, the staff, her mother, and I didn't know what to say to Krystal in response to her request. I knew there was nothing else I could do but be a listening presence. With the help of the wonderful question that had taken me many miles on my walks with the dying and those close to them, I queried both mother and daughter, "How may I help you?" The response was instantaneous. "Just walk with us, Cathy."

What a relief for me, as I didn't know what to do or say. As we walked along, I placed one hand over the hand Krystal's mother was using to push the high stroller and the other lightly on Krystal's shoulder.

The pediatric unit was shaped in a large oval with a core area in the center. The children's rooms formed a ring around the core. At one point, I spoke to Krystal and said that I knew she had to leave, but I wondered where she was going. This family did not have a tradition that included a sense of God, Heaven or the Hereafter.

Little Krystal answered that she was going far away and that it was dark there, but she quickly added, "Mommy has to go with me." After this exchange, her mother and I just held tightly to each other's hand and occasionally traded glances as we continued along, pushing Krystal and her ever-present IV pole around the circle.

Suddenly Krystal turned to us with an animated smile on her face and a sparkle in her eyes. She said, "It's all right, Mommy. You don't have to go with me." Both her mother and I were dumbfounded, relieved, and in shock—all at the same moment.

"Mommy doesn't have to go with you, Krystal?" I finally was able to say. "No, Cathy, Mommy doesn't have to go with me because where I'm going I'll be with Jimmy and Todd and Jennifer and Melissa," Krystal told us, while pointing to rooms as we circled the unit.

Krystal was naming children she knew who had been patients in the rooms we had passed. It was as if she were reading the small nameplates that were on the doors of the rooms these children had been in when they died. What was even more uncanny was that each child she named as she pointed to the rooms had in fact died of her type of leukemia. If only in her mind, these children had returned as Krystal's helpmates.

Lessons Reinforced

During this tiny patient's pain, confusion, and searching as her life came to an end, Krystal and her mother reinforced for me the importance of being a listening presence, mediator, translator, and educator. As you can imagine, I had traversed the ever-fluctuating hope system of both parent and child over the time they were in my care. I had accompanied them from intense hope for cure and hope for treatment, both supported through the rigors of experimental protocols, continuous tests, and a bone marrow transplant, to hope for prolongation of life, hoping for long-term remission until a cure for her type of leukemia was developed.

Because I was so clear on Krystal's hope system and my own for her, I was armed with clarity and strength. This enabled me to be present with her mother's pain, confusion, and feelings of utter helplessness—feelings which we both shared on each admission—to a degree that I had never before experienced in my work with the dying and their families. Thus, I was able to walk with them and hear Krystal say, "Mommy, you don't have to go with me."

My involvement in their hope journey continued with my helping Krystal prepare her mother by interpreting significant verbal, nonverbal, and behavioral changes. The interpretation of the verbal and nonverbal language of the dying is an important role for the professional caregiver when working with the dying, but is enhanced with dying children and their parents. It is only from the children themselves that the parent can hear and begin to accept that their child is really dying and leaving them.

Krystal's hope for a peaceful death was signaled very powerfully for me when I was dismissed by the dying child, who said, "That little girl over there who's crying needs you now, Cathy." In addition, Krystal had maturely told her elder sister that she was to "take care of Teddy [Krystal's stuffed animal] now and tuck him in at night. Don't let him get lonesome." In both of these powerful symbolic messages, Krystal clearly demonstrated her understanding and acceptance of her own hope for a peaceful death, indicating "I have to leave now."

The Take-Away for You

In this clinical example we see clearly demonstrated the trust relationship between Krystal, her family, and myself. I became the empty slate upon which Krystal wrote the final words of her life story in a way we were all able to understand and, thus, having understood, we were able to let her go.

Because I had taken the inward journey of my own personal hope system many times and was clear about what I hoped for Krystal at every step of her own process, I was able to be present to mother and child in the ways in which they needed me. I did not waver in my ability to be present because I was continually and consistently clear within myself. Consequently, I was free to be with them in their time of need.

For me and, I hope for you, this demonstrates very powerfully that we, as professional caregivers, do not have to have all the answers since the questions of life and death are often unanswerable. However, we must be willing to listen and to respond with the ever-changing hope systems of our patients and their loved ones so that we may walk with them as a true friend would, making contact eye to eye, then ear to ear, walking shoulder to shoulder with them, because it is not easy to let go and die, and finally connecting heart to heart, resonating with their hopes for life and death. By doing so, we will in fact be accompanying them on their final journey as they hope it will be.

****

What I have attempted to describe in this chapter is the evolution of hope within the patient, family, and professional caregiver, and the intricate ever-changing pattern and interaction that it creates. Hope is the dynamic life force that exists first within and then outside each person in relationship to self, environment, and their loved ones. Each of us possesses unique embodiments of hope, hope for ourselves, our families, our profession, and our world.

Acknowledging Your Own Hope System

Each of us as professionals has his or her own unique clinical knowledge, expertise, and competence. I invite you to take this uniqueness to a deeper level. Come to know and respect the individual resources of your own hope system. Take hold of this dynamic reality within you. Once it is yours, you will have the ability to respond and resonate with the needs and hopes of your patients and their families in a more real manner. This will enable you to establish and maintain therapeutic relationships at the highest level of your capabilities.

Take Care of Yourself

In order to take care of others we must take care of ourselves on all levels. To live a full and happy life when one deals daily with death and loss is truly a balancing act.

I have been able to work so long with the dying only because I work as hard at keeping my life in balance as I do on my work with the dying. I want to end this chapter by sharing with you some of the things which enable me to live a full and happy life:

- Sharing the burden—peer and staff support, process groups
- Meditation—quieting the mind
- Exercise—running, biking, walking, Tai Chi
- The beach or lake—healing water
- Retreats—silent, spiritual
- Dancing—freeing the spirit, fun
- Music—soothes the savage beast
- Nature—forest, mountains, hiking
- Being with children—playing
- Massage—manicure, body work

I hope that you find these suggestions helpful. The dying need energy and they will get it however they can. We need to remind ourselves everyday, "It is not my death. It is their death."

We each must die our own death. Yes, we are there to help them face their dying and death in a special and hopeful way. But we can't do it for them. What has enabled me to continue to be present for so many patients over the years is something I learned early on: I do my best, then, I let it go, for the outcome is not in my hands. Internalizing this phrase has helped me to be free to live my life fully.

Chapter 9

The Hand-Heart
Connection

Since the "letting go" of someone or the "giving permission" for that person to die is so difficult for loved ones to do, I would like to share with you something that I have learned which has helped both the dying and those near and dear to them.

Because the letting go and the subsequent separation appear to happen at the heart level, an approach I call "The Hand-Heart Connection" serves as a facilitator of the dying process, enabling both the dying and those close to them to "let go" in mutual release.

There is a direct relationship between the hand and the heart (in Eastern teachings, the heart is the fourth chakra or energy center). Thus, when we hold someone's hand, in a very special way, we are in fact holding his heart. In this we see an even deeper and more powerful reason and symbol for the commonly-seen practice of holding hands.

As the dying person comes nearer and nearer to death, we see the physical changes that indicate a marked decrease in his total life energy. These changes are manifested by increased weakness, lethargy, and even emaciation in some instances. He, in fact, seems to be fading away right in front of us. This—plus the other symbolic verbal and nonverbal behavior of the dying such as the cessation of speaking, eating, or even looking at those close to them—is very difficult for the family to endure, as fulfilling social and physical needs have been the family's primary ways of relating to and caring for this person.

What this often creates in those closest to the dying is an overwhelming feeling of helplessness, since they feel that they no longer have anything to offer the person, and they are losing contact with him even before his death occurs. This entire set of circumstances can bring on feelings of guilt, rejection, and abandonment before the person actually dies. These feelings are very powerful, and, on occasion, lead to behavior directly opposite to fulfilling the first basic need of the dying, which is that they will not be abandoned.

I have devised The Hand-Heart Connection to help families and other direct caregivers maintain necessary contact and to help decrease the feelings of helplessness and pain. This technique appears profoundly simple, but in reality it is simply profound. Just as touch was the primary mode of communication when we came into this world at birth, so too it remains the basic and most powerful medium of communication as we leave this world.

I will describe this approach in detail, as it has been one of the most effective and teachable tools to help those closest to the dying person to hold on, while they are in fact letting go, and to do this with less pain and more love. First, move to the left or heart side of the patient and place the patient's left hand gently in your own left hand, palm to palm. As the patient's hand sits in your upturned hand, begin to consciously think of and direct peace and love to the ill person, imaging tranquility and love filling and overflowing the dying person's heart.

Holding the hand is the connection and is all the contact that is necessary. Since this is an already-known and well-practiced action in many relationships, it is often something that anyone close to the dying feels comfortable doing. However, if you feel that you would like to increase this connection, here are some additional steps you may take.

After placing the person's left hand in your left hand (if it is inconvenient or awkward to hold his left hand, you may hold his right.), cover it with your right hand. This increases the sense of contact and security that the dying feels from you. I had a woman patient respond in a very special way to this touch. She awoke from an almost semicomatose state as I covered her hand with mine. Looking at me with bright eyes she said, "Oh, you're holding my heart!" and at that very moment, I had the sensation of a tiny heart beating in my hands as well.

If you are comfortable with it, gently move your right hand up the person's arm and place it on his left shoulder with your hand pointing to his heart. Again consciously send or direct peace and love to the heart of the dying person. The patient (who, we must remember, is not a passive participant in this interaction) may move your hand down nearer his heart, or perhaps place your hand in the center of his chest above the heart. I have seen many people do this as death comes closer and closer and they, although peaceful and accepting, become afraid of the unknown and of taking the final leap.

Fear Centers

This area in the center of the chest near the collarbone seems to be the place where fear lives in the dying. I compare it to the scared or panicky feeling we experience when we feel as though an elephant is sitting on our chest and we cannot breathe. Another area of fear or anxiety may be the area just below the stomach in the region of the solar plexus, which is often called the seat of emotion. It is in this area that we, throughout our lives, might have felt "butterflies" when confronted by a situation in which we felt afraid or experienced stress.

If either you or the patient are not comfortable with this hand placement, this can all be done from the back. Simply leave your hand on the left shoulder or place your hand in the center of the back at the chest and heart level and continue to send peace and love to him.

Breaking the Connection

When you feel that this connection is lessening, the loved one has loosened his grip on your hand, or you feel it's time to release the contact—perhaps the patient is sleeping soundly or you need to leave for awhile—it is important to remember that the disconnection is as important as the connection. If you have done the whole technique, simply retrace your steps, moving from the heart or chest area back to the left shoulder, and gently move your hand down his arm and place your right hand over his left hand, again cradling his hand (and heart) in your hands. Pause there and say or think your good-byes, tell him you love him, wish him peace, or say whatever comes to you. Then gently place the patient's hand back on the bed or on his lap.

As stated earlier, the simple act of holding the dying person's hand is sufficient to set this exquisite love connection into action. However, I have found it almost instinctual for the patient's loved ones to cover or cup their hands and gently touch or massage the upper back, neck, or shoulders as a way of maintaining contact or staying connected by touch with those whom they love.

This essential connection tends to decrease the tremendous feelings of helplessness felt by those closest to the dying.

Required Energy

An equally important reason for my devising this particular approach was to provide the dying person with the love and energy needed to complete this final life task. We utilize the heart in this approach for a very special reason, because it is here that separation and letting go must occur. The task of dying is separating from or letting go of all loved and known things and this, as we well know, is not an easy task, but one which requires energy. The dying person in fact loses life energy on all levels and therefore requires a tremendous influx of energy to complete the task of dying.

The Hand-Heart Connection helps provide the patient with the energy needed to release loved ones, especially those bonded by love and need. It can facilitate the saying of things previously left unsaid.

The Hand-Heart Connection also serves a very important third purpose. Because of the outgiving nature of the interaction, consciously directing peace to the dying, those staying behind are helped to let go via the flow of love and peace they are sending. This outflow of love energy helps them to loosen their grasp and relieves the feeling that they are abandoning the dying. They have, in fact, stayed in contact by maintaining a loving touch with them until the final separation we call death occurs.

The influx of love and life energy via The Hand-Heart Connection certainly can ease the dying process. It enables the dying to let go, while still having the feeling of being connected to and held onto by their loved ones. This connectedness insures the dying person that the basic need of not being abandoned is respected and honored until the end; it actually enables them to let go and die peacefully.

A Final Word

I believe that certain people come into our lives for a reason and that we are given opportunities through them to grow in ways that we would not have if their paths had not crossed ours. I have shared with you my own patients' voices and stories. Their wisdom was given to me and it has been my goal to pass it on to you. Please spread their wisdom to others who, at the difficult juncture when the Known meets the Unknown, may help make each dying person's transition more peaceful.

Resources

Resources for Family and Friends: Hospice, Palliative Care, and End-of-Life Care

Academy of Hospice and Palliative Medicine
    aahpm.org
Aging Parents and Elder Care
    aging-parents-and-elder-care.com
American Hospice Foundation
    americanhospice.org
Approaching Death: Improving Care at the End of Life
    nap.edu/readingroom/books/approaching
Barbara Ziegler Palliative Care Education Program
    Memorial Sloan-Kettering Cancer Center
    mskcc.org/zpep
Before I Die
    wnet.org/bid/index.html
 Caring Connections
    caringinfo.org
Center to Advance Palliative Care
    capc.org
Disparities at the End of Life
    rwjf.org
Elder Rage
    elderrage.com

End-of-Life Nursing Education Consortium (ELNEC)
    aacn.nche.edu/ELNEC/about.htm
End of Life Physician Education Resources (EPERC)
    eperc.mcw.edu
EndLink: Resources for End of Life Care Education
    endlink.lurie.northwestern.edu
Griefworks BC
    griefworksbc.com
Growth House, Inc.
    growthhouse.org
Hospice Foundation of America
    hospicefoundation.org
Legacies
    legacies.ca
Life's End Institute: Missoula Demonstration Project
    lifes-end.org
 NPR, The End of Life: Exploring Death in America
    npr.org
National Hospice and Palliative Care Organization
    nhpco.org
National Prison Hospice Association
    npha.org
 On Our Own Terms: Moyers on Dying Thirteen/WNET New York
    pbs.org/onourownterms
Promoting Excellence in End-of-Life Care
    promotingexcellence.org
Robert Wood Johnson Foundation
    rwjf.org
Share the Care
    sharethecare.org
Spiritual Care Program
    spcare.org
The National Center for Advanced Illness Coordinated Care
    coordinatedcare.net
Toolkit of Instruments to Measure End of Life Care
    chcr.brown.edu/pcoc/toolkit.htm

Support Services and Support Groups for Patients and Loved Ones Facing Chronic/Terminal Illness

American Cancer Society
    cancer.org/docroot/home/index.asp
American Heart Association
    americanheart.org
American Lung Association
    lungusa.org
Cancer Care
    cancercare.org

Resources for Professional Caregivers: Hospice, Palliative Care, and End-of-Life Care

Naropa University School of Extended Studies
    Contemplative End-of-Life Care: A Certificate Program for
    Healthcare Professionals
    naropa.edu/contemplativecare
National Hospice and Palliative Care Organization
    nhpco.org

Medical and Nursing Organizations Providing Education and Research for the Science and Art of End-of-Life Care

Academy of Hospice and Palliative Medicine
    aahpm.org
American Holistic Medical Association
    holisticmedicine.org
American Holistic Nuring Association
    ahna.org
Hospice and Palliative Nurses Association
    hpna.org
Oncology Nursing Society
    ons.org

Suggested Reading

Adding Value to Long-Term Care: An Administrator's Guide to Improving Staff Performance, Patient Experience, and Financial Health
Lazer, Dianne and Schwartz-Cassell, Tobi

Affirming the Darkness: An Extended Conversation About Living with Prostate Cancer
Wheeler, Chuck and Martha

All Kinds of Love: Experiencing Hospice
Jaffe, Carolyn and Ehrlich, Carol H.

An Ocean of Time: Alzheimer's Tales of Hope and Forgetting
Mathiasen, Patrick, M.D.

Another Morning: Voices of Truth and Hope from Mothers with Cancer
Blachman, Linda

By No Means: The Choice to Forgo Life-Sustaining Food and Water
Lynn, Joanne (editor)

Caring in Remembered Ways: The Fruit of Seeing Deeply
Davis, Maggie Steincrohn

Choices at the End of Life: Finding Out What Your Parents Want Before It's Too Late
Norlander, Linda, R.N., MS, and McSteen, Kerstin, R.N., MS

Companion to Grief: Finding Consolation When Someone You Love Has Died
Kelley, Patricia

The Courage to Laugh: Humor, Hope, and Healing in the Face of Death and Dying
Klein, Allen

Dancing With Mister D: Notes on Life and Death
Keizer, Bert

The Death of a Christian: The Order of Christian Funerals
    Rutherford, R. and Barr, T.

Death: The Trip of a Lifetime
    Palmer, Greg

The Denial of Death
    Becker, Ernest

A Different Kind of Health
    Justice, Blair, Ph.D.

The Diving Bell and the Butterfly
    Bauby, Jean-Dominique

Dying: A Book of Comfort
    McNees, P. (editor)

Dying At Home: A Family Guide for Caregiving
    Sankar, Andrea

Dying Well: The Prospect for Growth at the End of Life
    Byock, Ira, M.D.

Dying with Dignity: A Plea for Personal Responsibility
    Kung, Hans and Jens, Walter

Elder Rage—or—Take My Father... Please!
    Marcell, Jacqueline

*Facing Death and Finding Hope: A Guide for the Emotional and Spiritual
    Care of the Dying*
    Longaker, Christine

*Facing Death: Images, Insights, and Interventions: A Handbook for Educa-
    tors, Healthcare Professionals, and Counselors*
    Bertman, Sandra L.

Fading Away: The Experience of Transition in Families With Terminal Illness
    Davies, Betty, et al.

A Few Months to Live
    Staton, Jana; Shuy, Roger; and Byock, Ira, M.D.

Final Gifts: Understanding the Special Awareness, Needs, and Communica-
    tions of the Dying
    Callanan, Maggie and Kelley, Patricia

Forced Exit: The Slippery Slope from Assisted Suicide to Legalized Murder
    Smith, Wesley J.

The Four Things That Matter Most
    Byock, Ira, M.D.

The Gift of Peace: Personal Reflections
    Bernardin, Joseph Louis

The Gifts of the Body
    Brown, Rebecca

The Good Death: The New American Search to Reshape the End of Life
    Webb, Marilyn

Grace and Grit: Spirituality and Healing in the Life and Death of Treya
    Killam Wilber
    Wilber, Ken

Graceful Passages: A Companion for Living and Dying
    Malkin, Gary Remal and Stillwater, Michael

Grief and the Healing Arts
    Bertman, Sandra L. (editor)

A Grief Observed
    Lewis, C. S.

Grieving: A Love Story
    Coughlin, Ruth

Handbook for Mortals: Guidance for People Facing Serious Illness
    Lynn, Joanne, M.D., and Harrold, Joan, M.D.

Hard Choices for Loving People: CPR, Artificial Feeding, Comfort Measures Only and the Elderly Patient
    Dunn, Hank

The Healing Art of Storytelling
    Stone, Richard

The Healing Power of Creative Mourning
    Yager, Jan

The Helper's Journey: Working with People Facing Grief, Loss, and Life-Threatening Illness
    Larson, Dale G., Ph.D.

Helping Grieving People: When Tears Are Not Enough: A Handbook for Care Providers
    Jeffreys, Shep J., Ed.D.

Hospice Care for Children
    Armstrong-Dailey, Ann and Zarbock, Sarah (editors)

The Hospice Choice: In Pursuit of a Peaceful Death
    Lattanzi-Licht, Marcia; Mahoney, John J.; and Miller, Galen W.

The Hospice Handbook: A Complete Guide
    Berresford, Larry

How We Die: Reflections on Life's Final Chapter
    Nuland, Sherwin B.

I'm Here to Help: A Guide for Caregivers, Hospice Workers, and Volunteers
    Ray, Catherine

Illness as Metaphor and AIDS and Its Metaphors
    Sontag, Susan

Improving Care for the End of Life: A Sourcebook
    Lynn, Joanne; Lynch Schuster, Janice; and Kabcenell, Andrea

In the Shadow of Illness: Parents and Siblings of the Chronically Ill Child
    Bluebond-Langner, Myra, Ph.D.

Intimate Death: How the Dying Teach Us How to Live
    De Hennezel, Marie

Kitchen Table Wisdom: Stories that Heal
    Remen, Rachel N., Ph.D.

Last Rights: Rescuing the End of Life from the Medical System
    Kiernan, Stephen

Lean on Me: Cancer through a Carer's Eyes
    Kember, Lorraine

The Least of These My Brethren: A Doctor's Story of Hope and Miracles on an Inner City AIDS Ward
    Baxter, Daniel J., M.D.

Liberating Losses: When Death Brings Relief
    Elison, Jennifer, Ed.D., and McGonigle, Chris, Ph.D.

Life Worth Living: How Someone You Love Can Still Enjoy Life in a Nursing Home: The Eden Alternative in Action
    Thomas, William H., M.D.

It's All Good: Emails from a Dying Best Friend
    Widran, Jonathan

Living Our Dying: A Way to the Sacred in Everyday Life
    Sharp, Joseph

Living Posthumously: Confronting the Loss of Vital Powers
   Schmookler, Andrew B.

Living With Grief When Illness is Prolonged
   Doka, Kenneth, Ph.D., and Davidson, J. (editors)

*Living with Life-Threatening Illness: A Guide for Patients, Their Families,
   and Caregivers*
   Doka, Kenneth, Ph.D.

Long Goodbye: The Deaths of Nancy Cruzan
   Colby, William F.

Love is Stronger than Death
   Kreeft, Peter

Managing Death in the Intensive Care Unit: The Transition from Cure to Comfort
   Curtis, Randall J. and Rubenfeld, Gordon D. (editors)

Man's Search for Meaning
   Frankl, Victor E.

*Medical Care of the Soul: A Practical and Healing Guide to End-Of-Life
   Issues for Families, Patients, and Health Care Providers*
   Bartlow, Bruce G., M.D.

*A Midwife Through the Dying Process: Stories of Healing and Hard Choice at
   the End of Life*
   Quill, Timothy E., M.D.

More Than a Parting Prayer: Lessons in Care Giving for the Dying
   Griffith, William H.

Mortal Acts: Eighteen Empowering Rituals for Confronting Death
   Feinstein, David

Mortally Wounded: Stories of Soul Pain, Death, and Healing
   Kearney, Michael, M.D.

Mourning & Mitzvah: A Guided Journal for Walking the Mourner's Path Through Grief to Healing
     Brener, Anne, L.C.S.W

Mourning Has Broken: A Collection of Creative Writings about Grief and Healing
     Mara, Koven and Pearl, Liz

My Grandfathers Blessings: Stories of Strength, Refuge, and Belonging
     Remen, Rachel N., M.D.

My Own Country: A Doctor's Story
     Verghese, Abraham, M.D.

The Nature of Suffering and the Goals of Medicine
     Cassell, Eric J.

Nothing Left Unsaid: Creating a Healing Legacy with Final Words and Letters
     Polce-Lynch, Mary, Ph.D.

On Death and Dying
     Kübler-Ross, Elisabeth, M.D.

The Open Road: Walt Whitman on Death & Dying
     Vest, Joe (editor)

The Oxford Book of Death
     Enright, D.J. (editor)

Oxford Textbook of Palliative Medicine
     Doyle, Derek; Hanks, Geoffrey W.C.; and MacDonald, Neil (editors)

Palliative and End-of-Life Pearls
     Byock, Ira, M.D., and Heffner, John E.

Part of Me Died, Too: Stories of Creative Survival Among Bereaved Children and Teenagers
     Fry, Virginia Lynn

Patience, Compassion, Hope, and the Christian Art of Dying Well
Vogt, Christopher P.

Physician-Assisted Suicide
Weir, Robert F. (editor)

The Presence of the Dead on the Spiritual Path
Steiner, Rudolf

Raising Lazarus: A Memoir
Pensack, Robert Jon, M.D., and Williams, Dwight Arnan

Readings in Thanatology (Death, Value and Meaning)
Morgan, John D. (editor)

Refuge: An Unnatural History of Family and Place
Williams, Terry Tempest

R.I.P.: The Complete Book of Death and Dying
Jones, Constance

The Rights of the Dying: A Companion for Life's Final Moments
Kessler, David

Rituals for Living and Dying: From Life's Wounds to Spiritual Awakening
Feinstein, David and Mayo, Peg Elliot

Saying Goodbye to Daniel: When Death is the Best Choice
Rothman, Juliet Cassuto

Seduced by Death: Doctors, Patients, and the Dutch Cure
Hendin, Herbert, M.D.

Share the Care: How To Organize a Group to Care for Someone Who Is Seriously Ill
Capossela, Cappy; Warnock, Sheila; and Miller, Sukie

Signs of Life: A Memoir of Dying and Discovery
Brookes, Tim

The Singing Bird Will Come: An AIDS Journal
Noonan, John Richard

Six Months To Live: Different Paths to Life's End
Byock, Ira, M.D.; Staton, Jana; and Shuy, Roger

Stay Close and Do Nothing: A Spiritual and Practical Guide to Caring for the Dying at Home
Collett, Merrill

Surviving the Fall: The Personal Story of an AIDS Doctor
Selwyn, Peter A., M.D.

The Tibetan Book of Living and Dying
Rinpoche, Sogyal

A Time to Grieve: Meditations for Healing After the Death of a Loved One
Staudacher, Carol

To Live Until We Say Goodbye
Kübler-Ross, Elisabeth, M.D.

Tuesdays with Morrie
Albom, Mitch

The Troubled Dream of Life: In Search of a Peaceful Death
Callahan, Daniel

The Undertaking: Life Studies from the Dismal Trade
Lynch, Thomas

What the Dying Teach Us: Lessons on Living
Oliver, Samuel

When Bad Things Happen to Good People
    Kushner, Harold S.

When Life Becomes Precious: A Guide for Loved Ones and Friends of Cancer Patients
    Babcock, Elise NeeDell

Who Dies? An Investigation of Conscious Living and Conscious Dying
    Levine, Stephen

Words to Live By: A Journal of Wisdom for Someone You Love
    Marshall, Emily and Kate

The Wounded Storyteller: Body, Illness, and Ethics
    Frank, Arthur W.

You Can Help Someone Who's Grieving
    Frigo, Victoria; Fisher, Diane; and Cook, Mary Lou